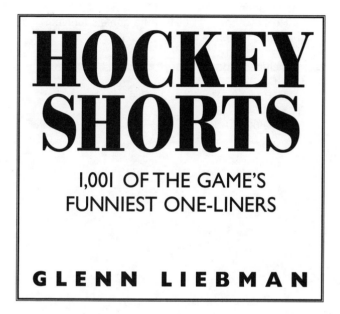

HOCKEY SHORTS

1,001 OF THE GAME'S FUNNIEST ONE-LINERS

GLENN LIEBMAN

CONTEMPORARY BOOKS

A TRIBUNE COMPANY

Library of Congress Cataloging-in-Publication Data

Liebman, Glenn.
    Hockey shorts : 1,001 of the game's funniest
one-liners / Glenn Liebman.
       p.   cm.
    Includes index.
    ISBN 0-8092-3351-7
    1. Hockey—Humor.   I. Title.
GV847.L54   1996
796.962'0207—dc20   96-7985
                                 CIP

Published by Contemporary Books
An imprint of NTC/Contemporary Publishing Company
Two Prudential Plaza, Chicago, Illinois 60601-6790
Manufactured in the United States of America
International Standard Book Number: 0-8092-3351-7
10   9   8   7   6   5   4   3   2   1

To my brother, Bennett.
As a friend, brother, fellow sports fanatic,
and former handicapper extraordinaire,
you are simply the best.

ACKNOWLEDGMENTS

As always, there are two people I can't thank enough, but I will attempt to, anyway: my agent, Philip Spitzer, who has been a great believer in and advocate for the Shorts series, and my editor, Nancy Crossman, without whose efforts there would be no Shorts series. Special thanks go to her for supporting and marketing the series so effectively.

I couldn't write a hockey book without acknowledging Billy Hanft and Victor Shimkin. It was my good fortune to grow up next door to Billy, who was like a second older brother to me. Among the best times of my childhood were the hockey games played in our basement every New Year's Day with Billy, my brother, Bennett, and other assorted friends and relatives. He was the scrappiest player I ever knew. He also had a pretty decent slap shot. I have many fond memories of times spent with Billy and his parents, Phoebe and Marcy ("Big Louie").

Victor Shimkin is the Gordie Howe of Albany. Whether facing a Tab Wilkins slap shot or a check from an opponent half his age, he is the best. The Ottawa Senators will be skating around with the Stanley Cup before Victor retires from the game.

I'd like to thank Sue and Dave Wollner and Scott Sommer—good friends with a lot of class—for reaching out to Kathy and me during this difficult period in our lives. And speaking of class, I'd also like to thank Helen and Jerry Klein, two of the nicest people I have ever met, who have become like family to us.

I would like to thank my dad, Bernie, who taught me to laugh at critics and smile at adversity, and my mom, Frieda, who through her love taught me to have a zest for life and a sense of humor. My brother, Bennett, as always, deserves a mountain of praise for his friendship, sense of humor, and generosity. He is also the father of the two cutest girls in the world—Samantha and Joy-Joy.

My mother-in-law, Helen Coll, as always, has served as an inspiration and a source of strength to all of us. She is a wonderful person.

My father-in-law, Bill Coll, showed me how to live a life devoted to family and friends. I will miss his friendship, compassion, and strength. I hope I can be half as good a person and father as he was.

The one and only Frankie Jay continues to be the funniest and cutest kid I ever knew (objectively speaking, of course). Whether it's bouncing a ball, saying a new word, or misplacing the TV remote control, he is the best!

I've saved the best for last. Thanks to my wonderful wife, Kathy, who told me eight years ago to follow my dreams and become a sportswriter. Simply put, she is the greatest person I ever met or ever will meet. (But you're still not getting new living-room furniture!)

INTRODUCTION

In 1974 I was in tenth grade. Even though I lived on Long Island, the guy who sat next to me in homeroom was the most obnoxious Boston Bruins fan in North America. He gave me 2–1 odds that year that the Bruins would beat the Flyers in the Stanley Cup finals.

The Flyers won that series 4–2. Not only did I win ten bucks, but I got this guy off my back. To pay back the Flyers, I became their number-one fan. My wall was filled with Bobby Clarke and Billy Barber posters. As a defenseman in street hockey, I always made believe I was Moose Dupont—no one could get around the Moose.

For the next ten years, I lived and breathed Flyers. I almost applied to colleges in Philadelphia just so I could be near the Spectrum.

Although my love for hockey remained, I eventually lost my passion for the Flyers. I switched my allegiance to the Rangers. After all, the Flyers had their two cups; the Rangers hadn't won a cup since the Jefferson administration.

The Rangers used to practice half an hour from where I live in upstate New York. Four years ago, I spent an entire week going to their practices. I had always heard that hockey players were the most approachable and least spoiled of all professional athletes. My experiences clearly confirmed this.

Mark Messier, one of the greatest to ever put on skates and Brian Leetch, the best defenseman in hockey, were more than willing to sign autographs. Almost every player was gracious and accommodating. The classiest of all was Adam Graves, who sat and talked with everyone. He and I spent fifteen minutes discussing the upcoming season.

This made that beautiful moment two years ago when the Rangers won the Stanley Cup even sweeter. Except for the Mets' miraculous comeback in the tenth inning of the '86 World Series, it was the greatest moment in sports for me since the Flyers beat the Bruins in '74.

Despite what the critics claim, hockey is a terrific sport to watch. There is something wonderful about the dichotomy between the brutal checking and the skating artistry. The game also lends itself to great personalities.

The most enjoyable part of this book was uncovering gems from hockey's funniest characters. Though my personal favorites were Bob Plager and Harry Neale, there seemed to be a special relationship between goalies and memorable one-liners. John Garrett, a perennial backup, after winning his first game of the season 10–9, said, "It was a good news–bad news type of situation. The good news is that we won; the bad news is that my average is 9.00."

Then there is the Jacques Plante classic: "Goaltending is a normal job." Sure! How would you like it in your job if every time you made a small mistake, a red light went on over your desk and 15,000 people stood up and yelled at you? Longtime goalie Reggie Lemelin said he knew it was time to retire "when a rookie asked me if he could take my daughter out on a date."

One of my favorite lines in the book comes from goalie Gump Worsley, one of hockey's great characters. One time when his coach admonished him for having a beer belly, Worsley replied, "He should know better than that. He knows I only drink Scotch."

With guys like Gumper, there was no lack of material for this book. So sit back, relax, and laugh along with hockey's funniest characters.

"He could deal with the peculiarities of youth."
Harold Ballard, on hiring Roger
Neilson for his young team

"I love it. I now get 10 percent off at the supermarket."
Johnny Bower, Hall of Fame goalie,
on turning 65

"He's as old as some trees."
Pat Burns, on the 36-year-old Mike
Gartner

"If they want me to play in the minors, I'll play. If they want me to play in China, I'll play. If they want me to play regularly, I'm in trouble."
Marcel Dionne, at the end of his
career

"I never felt so young coming to the rink."
Bob Froese, on the Flyers acquiring
37-year-old Chico Resch

"I'm fortunate it wasn't diaper rash."
> *Ted Green, Oilers coach, on young*
> *Jason Arnott being out with tonsillitis*

"It's tough when a defenseman is the same age as the owner."
> *Wayne Gretzky, on the Kings*
> *acquiring 39-year-old Larry Robinson*

"It's not a job anymore. It's a way of life."
> *Gordie Howe, on playing*
> *professionally at age 51*

"All I know is I have heartburn, I need sleep, and my feet hurt."
> *Mark Messier, asked how he felt*
> *about turning 30*

"He doesn't look like the paperboy. He looks like the paperboy's little brother."
> *Bryan Murray, on 21-year-old goalie*
> *Chris Osgood*

"I'm old and I'm tired, but I try my best."
> *Terry Sawchuck, after recording his*
> *103rd shutout at age 40*

"Old age."

Brian Sutter, asked what was the
ailment affecting Harold Snepsts

ALL—STAR GAME

"That's the problem with being picked for this
thing. You have to play."

Don Beaupre, after an All-Star Game
in which he gave up six goals

"I felt like a batting-practice pitcher out there. You
know, how they toss it up there and let the batters
crank it out of the ballpark."

Andy Moog, goalie, after playing in
an All-Star Game

"He only played two minutes. But they were a good
two minutes."

Roger Neilson, on John Garrett, who
was used as an All-Star Game
replacement for the Canucks' regular
goalie, Richard Brodeur, despite
having played only two minutes all
season

"The only way I'm going there is if my family stuffs the ballot box."

Bill Ranford, on his chances of making the 1990 All-Star Team

SYL APPS

"A Rembrandt on the ice, a Nijinsky at the goalmouth."

Vincent Lunny, on Syl Apps

ARBITRATION

"If you believed my side, I'm worth $2 million. If you believed theirs, I should be back in pee wee hockey."

Ken Wregget, on his arbitration case

"I've seen better ice on the roads in Saskatchewan."
Emile Francis, discussing the ice at
Madison Square Garden

"There's only going to be one Forum. This place is like a church for a lot of fans across Canada."
Guy Lafleur, on the Montreal Forum

"I'm not a romantic . . . about cockroaches and rats running around, no I am not."
Jacques Lemaire, asked how he felt
about the closing of Boston Garden

"In the other place, we were chasing cockroaches out of our stalls. You couldn't wait to get on the ice and get away from the cockroach house."
Jeremy Roenick, comparing Chicago
Stadium to the new United Center

ASSIST

"I think the whole game is to be played by a team, [and] the whole idea is to win. If someone is in the better position to score than I am, then I'm going to give him the puck."

Wayne Gretzky

"I didn't have a bonus for goals, so why not set up the guys who needed them?"

Doug Harvey, who was often accused of not shooting enough

ASSISTANT COACH

"I keep John Muckler's coffee hot, I get him a jelly doughnut, I count the players in the bus to make sure we're not leaving anyone behind, and I make sure we've got batteries for the walkie-talkies."

Ted Green, Oilers assistant coach

BACKUP

"It's like you're doing a good job at work and the other guy keeps getting the raise."

> *Allan Bester, on being the Maple Leafs' backup goalie despite 130 straight minutes of shutout netminding*

"It will be a lot easier sitting on the bench of a winning team than it is on a losing team."

> *John Garrett, backup goaltender*

"It's like I've been put in a closet and stored away."

> *Arturs Irbe, on being the third-string goalie for the San Jose Sharks*

HAROLD BALLARD

"He can fire me if he wants. But only if he has enough dough to buy this place."

> *Harold Ballard, on the powers he gave to new Toronto GM Gord Stellick*

"She doesn't pay me anything. I pay her. Besides, what position can she play?"

> *Harold Ballard, on tearing down a huge picture of the Queen hanging in Maple Leaf Garden to add more seats*

"I wish him luck wherever he goes."

> *Wendel Clark, after the death of the controversial Ballard*

"Mr. Ballard gives you the Chinese water torture until eventually you quit."

> *Gerry McNamara, former Toronto GM, on how you knew when your time with Toronto was up*

"Harold is a carnival."

> *Conn Smythe, on the many dimensions of Ballard*

"He is an old-fashioned buccaneer. If there's gold on a ship, it doesn't matter what flag you fly. Harold is going aboard to get the gold."

> *Stafford Smythe, former partner of Ballard*

"He was the opposite of most people. Pleasant on the inside, negative on the outside."
Gord Stellick

"It's like going out with the best-looking girl in high school. You know she's going to dump you eventually. But still, you've got to go for it."
Gord Stellick, on being the Maple Leafs' GM under Ballard

BASEBALL

"Guys strike out all the time in baseball, but if a goalie misses one, the world is over."
Murray Bannerman

"I'll stick to my job."
Wayne Gretzky, asked how he would feel about facing a Dwight Gooden fastball

"When he was playing hockey, he only showed up every five days too."

> *Barry Long, on former hockey player and major league baseball pitcher Kirk McCaskill*

BED REST

"I wondered whether I had one of those vibrating beds. If so, they must have put a dollar in instead of a quarter."

> *Craig Muni, Oilers player, following an earthquake in Montreal*

JEAN BELIVEAU

"It was like running into the side of a big oak tree. I bounced right off the guy and landed on the seat of my pants."

> *Bill Ezinicki, on attempting to check Beliveau*

"I've got news for you. We all do."

Terry Sawchuck, on an exhibition in which a sports reporter closed his eyes when Beliveau took a shot

BETTIN' MAN

"If I knew the answer to that, I'd bet $10,000 on the game and retire from coaching."

Toe Blake, asked if the Canadiens were going to win an upcoming game

"If I were a gambling man and I saw Bruce Hood refereeing a game involving our team, I'd have to bet against the Bruins. And I'd win just about every time."

Don Cherry

BEVERAGE OF CHOICE

"It was a beer-drinking crowd. In Texas, they measure distance by six-packs. You ask how far it is from here to there and they say, 'Oh it's a six-pack ride or it's a two-six-pack ride.'"

> *Randy Carlyle, on playing in Dallas in 1976 when it was the home of Toronto's minor league team*

"It wasn't that I drank so much, it's just that I put it into such a small body."

> *Bobby Sheehan, on his legendary drinking antics*

"He should know better than that. He knows I only drink Scotch."

> *Gump Worsley, after being accused by his coach of having a beer belly*

BLACKHAWKS

"The Blackhawks—no Europeans and no face shields."

> *Don Cherry, asked who his favorite NHL team was*

"Sometimes our fans cheer opposing goals."

> *John Marks, on a bad Blackhawks team*

"They can all go jump in a lake. There's a big lake here."

> *Orval Tessier, after the Blackhawks lost 6–2 to the Sabres in Buffalo*

BLUES

"The Ralston-Purina Company treated us as though we were a division of green beans and puppy chow."

> *Blake Dunlop, Blues forward, on the team being owned by Ralston-Purina*

MIKE BOSSY

"I couldn't possibly prepare for that move. All I could think to myself was, 'Which one of his 150 moves is Mike Bossy going to use this time?'"
Michel Dion

"What I want for Christmas is a Mike Bossy doll. Wind it up and he scores 60 goals."
Tom McVie

"Bossy scores goals as naturally as you and I wake up in the morning and brush our teeth."
Chico Resch

RAY BOURQUE

"Raymond's so strong and fast, I'd like to see him go a mile and a half on the turf in a stakes race."
Gerry Cheevers

"I don't want to take him out of the game, because I want to be able to watch him play."
Mike Milbury

"Ray can carry a game and never touch the puck."
Andy Moog, on Bourque's leadership qualities

"If I'm down a goal late in the game, I want Orr on the ice. If I'm up a goal late in the game, Bourque's the one I want out there."
Harry Sinden

SCOTTY BOWMAN

"He is complex, confusing, misunderstood, unclear in every way but one: He is a brilliant coach."
Ken Dryden

BOXING

"Ali comes to meet Semenko,
but Semenko's starting to retreat.
If Semenko goes back an inch further,
he'll end up in a ringside seat."

> *Muhammad Ali, on an exhibition*
> *fight against Dave Semenko*

"I don't want nothing coming at me that I can't
stop."

> *Joe Frazier, heavyweight champ, on*
> *goaltending*

BREAKAWAY

"Guy Lafleur flies down the ice. Steve Shutt soars.
Bob Gainey barrels. I sort of crash."

> *Terry O'Reilly*

"I told him you missed the most exciting 10 minutes in the history of the building. One night I had a breakaway."

> *Bob Plager, on giving advice to a guy who was writing a book about the history of the St. Louis Arena*

BRUINS

"What are you going to call the Bruins—the Cuddly Bears?"

> *Kevin McHale, after hearing that hockey's Anaheim franchise would be nicknamed the Mighty Ducks*

BUSINESS

"We weren't wrapped up with agents and all that business. Frankly, I don't know whether it was dedication to the sport or that we were just damned fools."

> *Frank Boucher, on hockey in the old days*

CANADA CUP

"It's sort of like seeing your mother-in-law on the edge of a cliff in your new Mercedes-Benz."

> *Dale Tallon, on players like Gretzky playing for Canada in the Canada Cup series against the United States*

CANADA / RUSSIA CUP

"Canada to romp in eight . . . it's a Russian team in decay."

> *Dick Beddoes, Toronto Globe reporter, before the '72 series, which went the full eight games, Canada barely winning in the last few minutes of the final contest*

"If someone gave the Russians a football, they'd win the Super Bowl in two years."

> *Frank Mahovlich, marveling at how the Russians came close to beating the Canadians in the '72 series*

"When people call my name, I don't duck like I used to."

> *Arthur Griffiths, Canucks owner, on the team's rise to prominence*

"I've been to games there in which you could sit in the stands and hear the players talking amongst themselves on the ice."

> *Scotty Morrison, Head of NHL Officials, on the early days of NHL play in Vancouver*

"It's not hard to jump on a corpse."

> *Harry Neale, on a barrage of goals scored against his Canucks team by Edmonton*

CAR TALK

"Tonelli's the Chevy with all the hard miles. The way he plays wears you down."

> *Terry Crisp, on the tenacious play of John Tonelli*

"I'm a 1978 Toyota with 86,000 miles on it, rust spots, and a hole in the floorboard. But hey, I start every morning."

> *Mike Milbury, in 1987*

"If he can handle that hit, he can handle anything in the NHL."

> *Harry Neale, on Petr Klima's car being totaled on the autobahn*

'CAUSE YOU'VE GOT PERSONALITY

"A bar in Chicago asked him to leave because they wanted to have Happy Hour."

> *Bob Plager, on the never-smiling Vaclav Nedomansky*

"Patrick wasn't tight with money, he was adjacent to it."

> *Babe Pratt, on Rangers coach Lester Patrick*

"When I played for Lester Patrick in New York, he wouldn't give a worm to a blind bird."
> *Babe Pratt*

"Lester, now I'm being paid enough to eat on. I'm finally getting the wrinkles out of my belly."

> *Babe Pratt, on no longer having to deal with his nemesis and former coach Lester Patrick*

"Tobin is so cheap that he wouldn't pay 10 cents to see the Statue of Liberty take a swan dive into New York Harbor."

> *Conn Smythe, on Bill Tobin, Blackhawks GM in the 1940s and '50s*

CHEATER

"Do they think this is the World Wrestling Federation or something?"

> *Ray Bourque, on accusations that he*
> *bit a blood capsule so the Canadiens*
> *would be assessed a major penalty*

"Everyone cheats in hockey. It's unbelievable how much you can get away with if you do it when no one is looking, or cares."

> *Tom Lysiak*

CHECKMATE

"Hey, Busher, how long those goddamned orders for?"

> *John Gagnon, Canadian star of the*
> *'30s, after Harvey Busher Jackson*
> *checked him hard all game but told*
> *him not to take it personally because*
> *he was just following coaches orders*

"Either you give it right back or the next thing you know, everybody and his brother will be trying you on for size."

Doug Harvey, on tough checks

"Our best system of forechecking is to shoot the puck and leave it there."

Harry Neale, on a bad Canucks team

CHRIS CHELIOS

"He's a junkyard dog who makes a million dollars."

Pat Burns, on Chelios

"He's just a lousy person. He never goes after tough guys. He just goes after guys who don't fight."

Brian Propp

"Chicago—the home of Michael Jordan, Bobby Hull, Stan Mikita, and Al Capona."

> *Bobby Holik, offering his impressions on his rookie year after coming over from Czechoslovakia*

"I went to a restaurant in such a rough neighborhood in Chicago that they have a no-shooting section."

> *Harry Neale*

BOBBY CLARKE

"Leadership is Bobby's desire to win. He does so much, so well. Listen, he'd drive the ice-cleaning machine if they wanted him to."

> *Terry Crisp*

"The rest of us are all retired and up in the press box and he's still out there. I think the little bugger got a body transplant."

Bernie Parent, on the 33-year-old Clarke

THE CLASSICS

"A coloring book that Joey hasn't finished."

Kelly Chase, asked to name Joey Kocur's favorite book

"Three years ago I couldn't spell author. Now I are one."

Don Cherry, on his autobiography

CLOTHESHORSE

"Jacket 42 Long. Leave extra room for biceps."

Glen Hanlon, on the size suit he was to wear for a benefit

"I learned a long time ago from Sam Pollock that you take a lot of aggravation from a .300 hitter that you wouldn't with a .200 hitter."

> *Scotty Bowman, on dealing with the often difficult Real Cloutier*

COACHING

"Coaching is aggravation. You give the players aggravation and they give it back."

> *Al Arbour*

"Twice as good. But what's two times zero?"

> *Herb Brooks, asked if he was a better coach with the North Stars than he was with the Rangers*

"Coaching is like being king. It prepares you for nothing."

> *Herb Brooks*

"If I did I don't know what I'd put in there. Maybe some socks and some underwear."

> *Gerry Cheevers, wondering why other NHL coaches carried briefcases*

"I don't score any points, I don't play on defense, and I'm not a goalkeeper."

> *Jacques Demers, asked to explain the significance of his 100th win as a coach*

"When I was a coach, I couldn't be one of the boys. This way, if I want a beer with them, I get a beer."

> *Doug Harvey, on why he was a coach for only a short time*

"If your good players don't play to the best of their ability, I don't give a damn if you're Toe Blake, you're not going to win."

> *Paul Holmgren, after being fired as Flyers coach*

"I think a coach has to be like a gardener. Some guys need weeding, some guys need watering, some need sunlight and some just need a Weedwacker."

> *Paul Holmgren*

"There are times when I may as well be up in the stands having a cup of coffee with the press for all the control I have."

Bob Johnson

"I was reading the *Hockey News* before the season started—Defense, D-plus, Forwards, D-plus. I was afraid to look. I closed it before I got to the coaching."

Doug MacLean, Panthers coach, after his team got off to a great start

"I can be out of town in 20 minutes, 30, if I have stuff at the cleaners."

Tom McVie, on his frequent moves as an NHL coach

"This isn't microbiology. I've been in the game 16 years and should have figured out something."

Mike Milbury, after being named Coach of the Year

"I guess it's why you never say never. The only thing you can never do is ski through a revolving door."

> *Lou Nanne, on coaching the North Stars after vowing never to coach again*

"Coaching is like running a restaurant. You cook one bad meal and everyone tells eight others about it. Cook a good meal and no one tells anyone."
> *Pierre Page*

"If I'm half the coach on the bench that I was in the stands, we'll have no problems."
> *Bob Plager*

"The difference between the NHL and the NBA is, if you're in last place in the NBA, they fire the coach. If you're in last place in the NHL, they give you a roast."

> *John Salley, at a roast for Jacques Demers, coach of the last-place Red Wings*

"When you're a coach, you're miserable. When you're not a coach, you're more miserable."
> *Fred Shero*

"You can't sleep at night, you can't eat properly, your hair turns gray. But boy is it fun."

Terry Simpson, former Islanders coach

"He scored hockey by the number of fights. If you lost 7 to 1, but won five fights, he figured you won the game."

Conn Smythe, on why King Clancy was a lousy coach

"Good luggage."

Glen Sonmor, on what is needed to accept a coaching job in hockey

PAUL COFFEY

"He's the only guy I've seen who can accelerate when he's coasting."

Harry Neale, on Coffey

"Only if I learn to play the organ."
> *Pierre Bouchard, asked if he wanted*
> *to return to the NHL*

"They say you're only as good as your last game.
But I can't remember mine."
> *John Garrett, Oilers commentator, on*
> *being asked to possibly play after a*
> *five-year hiatus when both Oilers*
> *goaltenders got hurt*

"He's had more comebacks than Muhammad Ali."
> *Harry Neale, on the oft-injured Glen*
> *Hanlon*

COMMISSIONER

"A know-nothing shrimp."
> *Harold Ballard, on John Ziegler*

"As a commissioner, you are almost like an official. From the start, everything is against you and you'd better understand that."

Clarence Campbell

"There is nothing so past as a past president."

Clarence Campbell

"If John Ziegler were alive, this never would have happened."

Bob Verdi, columnist, on the short-lived 1992 players' strike

"I gave Gary a hockey puck once, and he spent the rest of the day trying to open it."

Pat Williams, on Gary Bettman, who had little hockey experience before becoming commissioner

CONTRACTS

"Howard, we must renegotiate."

> *Gordie Howe, to Whalers owner*
> *Howard Baldwin after the roof of the*
> *Hartford Civic Center collapsed in*
> *1978. Baldwin had promised that*
> *Howe would be under contract with*
> *Hartford till the roof caved in.*

CORNER MAN

"I hope they bury me in the corner part of the cemetery, because if I'm in a corner, I'll be able to rest in peace forever."

> *Wayne Cashman*

"It was easy for the Commies to hide. They just put their boats in the corner of the harbor, because everyone knows Swedes don't go in corners."

> *Don Cherry, on the Russians moving*
> *submarines into the harbor in*
> *Stockholm*

"To me being tough includes going into corners without phoning ahead to see who's there."
Ted Lindsay

CREASE

"You could have a house party with 200 people and have more room than you have in the crease."
Grant Fuhr

"Trying to keep him out of the crease is like trying to tackle a jaguar. Not the animal—the car."
Ron Greschner, on Tim Kerr

CRIME AND PUNISHMENT

"If you got a chance to screw the government out of a few bucks, you'd do it too."
Harold Ballard, after being arrested for tax evasion

"I imagine some prisoners at Millhaven eat much better than the average Canadian."

Harold Ballard, on Millhaven penitentiary, where he was incarcerated after tax-evasion charges

DEAD AND BURIED

"I thought you have to be dead to have your number retired."

Steve Duchesne, on having his number retired by his junior hockey league team

"You're not supposed to still be alive, are you?"

Wayne Gretzky, on a statue of him being built in Edmonton

"At that age, everybody thinks they know what's best. By the time you realize what your father was telling you was true, your own kids are telling you you're wrong."

Wayne Gretzky, on the headstrong Eric Lindros at age 18

"My father could put green vegetables on the table even when he ran down coyotes barehanded and got a 10-dollar bounty for the tail. He was really a great athlete."

Gordie Howe

DEE—FENSE

"I'm down on the floor working in the pit. It's like being a defenseman standing in front of the net—a lot of pushing, shoving, elbowing, sweating, and cursing going on."

Jack O'Callahan, comparing his hockey career with his current job in the stock exchange

"I told him not to worry. I brush my teeth every day."

> *Esa Tikkanen, on shadowing Craig Janney during the 1990 playoffs*

"Defensively, we ran around like pregnant foxes in a forest fire."

> *Tom Watt, former Canucks coach, after his team gave up several goals in a game*

DEVILS

"We can beat those guys any day."

> *Harold Ballard, bragging about his Maple Leafs team, who had the same 22–40–6 record as the Devils*

"In the face-offs, I'm going to call everyone a loser, which is what they've been calling me for 14 years."

> *Bobby Carpenter, on finally winning the Stanley Cup as a member of the Devils*

"They are running a Mickey Mouse operation on the ice."

> *Wayne Gretzky, on the Devils during their early years*

"If you don't like our style, well, too bad, go watch a show somewhere else."

> *Claude Lemieux, on the Devils' defense-oriented style*

"When we lose, I get letters from religious organizations. They say until you change the name of the Devils to the Angels, you'll keep on losing."

> *John McMullen, Devils owner*

"They've got the wrong Larmer [Jeff], the wrong Trottier [Rocky], and the wrong Broten [Aaron]."

> *Walt McPeck, sportswriter, on the Devils*

"I guess I'm supposed to ride in on a white horse and deliver. But you can't expect me to come in here and do it alone, even though Paladin did. Those Western towns were smaller."

> *Tom McVie, on taking over the reins of the Devils*

"I guess if I let in a bad goal, I can shake it off by saying the Devil made me do it."

> *Chico Resch, on the Colorado Rockies moving to New Jersey and calling themselves the Devils*

DINO

"He's like a fly that won't go away. He's buzzing around your nose and mouth, you keep swatting at him, but he won't go away."

> *Neil Sheehy, on Dino Ciccarelli*

MARCEL DIONNE

"Everybody's been calling me and asking me when I'm going to do it. If I knew, I'd tell my wife and we'd win the trip."

> *Marcel Dionne, after the Kings announced a prize of a trip to England for anyone who could predict when Dionne would eclipse Phil Esposito's scoring record*

"When he put his arms out to celebrate, the rest of us skated immediately to the bench and left him there all alone."

Dave Taylor, on Marcel Dionne receiving death threats before a game in which he scored two goals

DIRTY POOL

"There are 26 general managers, and 25 complain about him. And all 25 would take him in a heartbeat."

Brian Burke, league VP, on Ulf Samuelsson

"The lowest form of human being. I wouldn't want him on my team. He has no honor."

Don Cherry, on Ulf Samuelsson

"He who lives by the cheap shot dies by the cross-check."

Stan Fischler

"Number one, I don't like him. Number two, I'd love to have him on my club."

Ted Green, on Ulf Samuelsson

"Hey, it's a man's game. If you can't play, get out and play tennis."

Bryan Marchment, on his reputation as one of hockey's dirtiest players

"There are rough players and there are dirty players. I'm rough and dirty."

Stan Mikita

"Jerk that he is, he's always wearing that smirking grin that makes you want to punch him in the face."

Mike Milbury, on Ulf Samuelsson

"If they had a poll of players, he'd win as the dirtiest player in the league. Nobody else is close. I hate the guy."

Bernie Nicholls, on Ulf Samuelsson

"Can you vote for yourself?"

> *Ulf Samuelsson, on being voted by a poll of 56 players as the dirtiest in the league*

"I'd give him a bonus."

> *Mathieu Schneider, asked what he thought Tie Domi deserved for sucker-punching Ulf Samuelsson*

DISCO INFERNO

"We led the league in binoculars."

> *Bob Plager, on six young women who regularly disco-danced in the stands at the St. Louis Checkerdome*

"I'm going to go into the locker room and dive into the Cup."

> *Mario Lemieux, after Mike Keenan*
> *accused him of taking dives during*
> *the '92 finals against Chicago*

"If Herbie ever decides he doesn't want to coach hockey anymore, I'm sure he can get a bathing suit and coach the Olympic diving team. He certainly taught those players of his how to take a dive or two."

> *Bob McCammon, on Herb Brooks*

"I think instead of sending players to power-skating school, we will send them to acting school."

> *Bob McCammon, on all the dives*
> *taken in the NHL*

DIVISION RACE

"It's a lot like puppy love. Nobody else takes it seriously, but it's real to the puppies."

Jimmy Devellano, on the awful
Norris Division of the mid-1980s

"You win a game in this division and you think about finishing in first place. Lose one, and you worry about finishing last."

Roger Neilson, on the mediocre
Patrick Division of 1990

DIVORCE

"If our goalies were in a divorce case, they could sue for lack of support and be millionaires tomorrow."

Terry Crisp, after his Tampa Bay
Lightning lost 10–0 to the Flames

"It's like divorcing yourself from 20 wives."

Glen Sather, on leaving as head
coach of the Oilers

DON'T WORRY, BE HAPPY

"As a coach, you know you are going to be fired, and as a player, you know you are going to get traded, so why worry about it."
>*Pierre Page*

"I want to be miserable. That makes me happy. In other words, I think you can't know joy if you don't know sorrow."
>*Fred Shero*

DOWN THE TOILET

"It may not be as exciting to flush your toilet as to watch NHL hockey, but it's a lot more essential."
>*Roger Young, Winnipeg City councilman, debating whether the city should help finance the Jets or a new sewer system*

DRAFT CHOICE

"Having a goon-type player is like having a water bottle sit on the bench and pay it $100,000 a year and squirt it at people once in a while."

> *Shawn Antoski, denying that he was a goon after being drafted No. 1 by the Canucks*

"I've got his name up on a board in my bedroom. I sleep with his name right close by, hoping it rubs off by osmosis or something."

> *Lou Nanne, on Minnesota's attempt to trade for the No. 1 pick in the draft—Brian Bellows*

"Draft picks have a way of ending up as bartenders."

> *Darryl Sutter, on his aversion to trading star players for draft choices*

KEN DRYDEN

"A thieving giraffe."

> *Phil Esposito, on the great*
> *goaltending skills of Dryden*

RON DUGUAY

"How would you like to go home and see Ron Duguay's picture on your wife's dressing table?"

> *Herb Brooks, on the pressure he felt*
> *as the Rangers' coach for benching*
> *Duguay*

EDUCATION

"I'm the first man in my family in five generations who didn't get a doctorate in anything. I guess I'm still working on my master's in hockey."

> *Jeff Brubaker*

"If I ever see him read a book on the bus again, I'm going to throw him off."

> *Emile Francis, on college graduate*
> *Red Berenson*

"There were at least two pterodactyl in there."

> *Ken Hammond, RPI grad, asked if*
> *he had butterflies in his stomach*
> *before his first game*

"You can't stay in high school forever. You've got to leave and go to the university."

> *Pierre Page, on leaving his job as a*
> *Flames assistant coach to take over*
> *as the North Stars' head coach*

"Maybe I couldn't read books, but I sure learned to listen to guys who did."

> *Eddie Shack, on being wealthy*
> *despite his lack of formal education*

"He's a Boston College kid. He was brought up right—right from the start."

> *Kevin Stevens, BC grad, on new*
> *teammate Joey Mullen*

"Me on instant replay."

> *Derek Sanderson, asked to name the*
> *greatest player he ever saw*

ENTERTAINMENT NEWS

"As much as I love hockey, there's more to life than sitting in the stands trying to avoid being hit by a puck."

> *Janet Jones, Wayne Gretzky's wife, on*
> *going back to pursue her acting*
> *career*

"We followed Tina around for a couple of days and now we've caught up with Whitney. I have to say, though, it's not bad company."

> *Don MacAdam, Red Wings assistant*
> *coach, on canceling practice in*
> *Vancouver because of a Whitney*
> *Houston concert, after canceling*
> *practice in Edmonton for a Tina*
> *Turner concert the week before*

"We could use her on our team. She'd improve our appearance and she works her butt off."

> *Harry Neale, after seeing Tina*
> *Turner in concert*

"Having him on the power play is like putting Cheryl Tiegs at middle linebacker."

> *Eric Nesterenko, after working with*
> *Rob Lowe on the movie* Youngblood

ESPO

"Jesus saves and Esposito scores on the rebound."

> *Anonymous, famous saying in Boston*
> *during the days of Phil Esposito*

"If I could have Phil Esposito, I'd put the Stanley Cup in my station wagon and go on tour with it."

> *Harold Ballard*

"You'd see Phil in front of you in the slot in the power play, shooting and shooting, and you'd say, 'Doesn't he ever get tired? Won't his arms fall off?' He'd scare me."

> *Ken Dryden*

"I'd buy Phil Esposito with my own money if I could, and I'd rent him to the Sabres."

> *Punch Imlach, during his days as*
> *Sabres GM*

"I'll tell you how good Phil Esposito is. When you're going against Espo, you start at least one goal down."

> *Punch Imlach*

"Phil rents the slot from the Boston Garden."

> *Bobby Orr*

EXPANSION

"You gotta sleep before you have nightmares."

> *Bep Guidolin, asked if he had*
> *nightmares as coach of the expansion*
> *Kansas City Scouts*

"Not Cleveland—God, no."

> *Peter Karmanos, Whalers owner, on*
> *possible expansion sites*

"War is hell, but expansion is worse."
Tom McVie

FACE-OFF

"I'm a hockey player, not a fashion model."
Shayne Corson, asked how he looked
after getting 40 stitches in his face

"I don't know, I never felt his nose."
Gordie Howe, asked if he thought
Reg Fleming was a hard-nosed player

"If he ever scored 50, I'd hate to see what he'd look like."
Tom Johnson, on Craig Janney, after
Janney got his first NHL goal off a
deflection to his eye

"We get nose jobs all the time in the NHL, and we don't even have to go to the hospital."
Brad Park

"What were you trying to do, shoot until you got Blue in the face?"

> *Peter Schwartz, reporter, on Steve Thomas's shot that hit goalie John Blue in the helmet*

"It's the first time a ref called me into the face-off circle to tell me I had lipstick on my face."

> *Doug Wilson, on being kissed by his wife before his 1,000th NHL game*

FAMILY AFFAIR

"When I heard the boos, the first thing I did was look in the stands and make sure my wife and daughter were clapping."

> *Scotty Bowman, after being booed in his first home game after the Red Wings were swept by the Devils in the Stanley Cup finals*

"See them? If you don't play well, I get fired."

> *Colin Campbell, Rangers coach, showing star forward Alexei Kovalev a picture of his family*

"Her hardest job is not to keep smiling when she drops me off at the airport."

Don Cherry, on his wife Rose

"Georges probably figured that playing goal in the NHL was the quietest spot in his life. After all, he was the father of 22 children."

King Clancy, on Georges Vezina

"We went the animal route. It cost more to feed them but not as much to educate them."

Glen Hanlon, explaining why he and his wife have a dog, a cat, and a horse but no kids

"I guess I'm the last of the line. The old name has just petered out."

Pete Peeters, on naming his son Jeremy, ending three generations of sons named Pete

FAN MAIL

"I used to get letters from women. Now I get letters from seven-year-old boys who say I'm their favorite player—and their mothers love me too."
Harold Snepsts

"Ever since then, I've always read my mail."
Glen Sonmor, North Stars coach, on a letter he received from a fan suggesting he wear an eye patch to end the team's 14-game losing streak to the Bruins in Boston. He wore the patch and his team won the game.

"I'm enjoying everything except when people put 'Ms.' on the envelope of my letters."
Kay Whitmore, Whalers goalie

FANS

"They should put the protective glass all the way to the ceiling there."
Rick MacLeish, on the Rangers' fans

"This is ridiculous. You coach for three games and they give you a night."

> *Joe Watson, honored by Philadelphia*
> *fans for his years as a Flyer, a*
> *ceremony that coincided with his*
> *taking over temporarily as coach*
> *while Pat Quinn served a three-game*
> *suspension*

SERGEI FEDEROV

"He's learning the North American way: Get greedy, score goals, get paid."

> *Bryan Murray*

"He makes goalies eat hockey pucks like Ring Dings."

> *Steve Rushin, sportswriter*

"The fans love fighting. The players don't mind. The coaches like the fights. What's the big deal?"
Don Cherry

"I socked Eddie once as he was getting to his feet and skated like mad to the other end of the rink."
> *King Clancy, on how he beat up the much stronger and tougher Eddie Shore*

"I went to a fight the other night and a hockey game broke out."
Rodney Dangerfield

"If they took away our sticks and gave us brooms, we'd still have fights."
Phil Esposito

"Hockey is 60 minutes of action with no easy way of avoiding a good clobbering."
Emile Francis

"He hit me on the head with his stick. And he didn't apologize."

> Rod Gilbert, on why he fought with Bill Lesuk

"In the big games, we try to beat the other guys up."

> Ted Green

"Sometimes people ask, 'Are hockey fights for real?' I say, 'If they weren't, I'd get in more of them.'"

> Wayne Gretzky

"I would have bled all over him."

> Wally Hergesheimer, after clinching with tough guy Bob Armstrong and being asked what would have happened had they fought

"I feel right at home being here with all these hockey players. Of course, I've always enjoyed entertaining the fighting men."

> Bob Hope

"You take fighting out of the game, it would really make it dull."

Gordie Howe

"A good fighting club will beat a club that has superstars on it every time."

Punch Imlach

"If you see European hockey, there are no fights, and it's boring."

Eddie Johnston

"Before we only fought over who should clean the house."

Joey Kocur, after an on-ice fight with former friend and teammate Bob Probert

"Sometimes I think I enjoy it. I think they didn't call me up from the minors because I scored six goals."

Joey Kocur, on being called up by the Red Wings in midseason because of his fighting ability

"I do know this about fighting in the NHL right now. As a tactic, it works."

Lou Lamoriello

"I thought I was at a hockey game."

Mario Lemieux, after throwing out the first ball at a Pirates–Expos game during which a fight broke out

"Next thing you know, they'll have us in dresses, in nylons with a pink garter."

Kevin McClelland, on a new rule stipulating that fights would mean automatic ejection from the game

"When you win a real pressure game with a lot of fights, you go home and you feel a little closer to your teammates. The fights make it a real spiritual game."

Marty McSorley

"The last time two things that big got together, Secretariat was born."

Harry Neale, on a fight between big guys Paul Cavallini and John Kordic

"I just wanted to let him know we hadn't forgotten."

> *Terry O'Reilly, on tripping Wilf*
> *Paiement who two weeks earlier had*
> *broken the jaw of O'Reilly's*
> *teammate Charlie Simmer*

"Go out there, and don't dance."

> *Don Perry, Kings coach, sending*
> *Paul Mulvey out to fight. Mulvey*
> *refused and was immediately put on*
> *waivers.*

"It's not who wins the fight that's important, it's being willing to fight. If you get challenged and renege, everyone wants to take a shot at you."

> *Barclay Plager*

"I fought in bars when I was 16, on the streets when I was 17, and on the ice everywhere from that point on."

> *Bob Plager*

"I'm low on sticks and didn't want to lose one on his head."

> *Mike Richter, on not swinging at Tie Domi, who had sucker-punched Richter's teammate Ulf Samuelsson*

"There never has been a death attributed to a hockey fight. Why don't they write about the good things for a change?"

> *Fred Shero*

"It was pretty much a 50-50 proposition. You socked the other guy and the other guy socked you."

> *Eddie Shore, on hockey in the old days*

"If we don't put a stop to it, we'll have to start printing more tickets."

> *Conn Smythe, on fighting in hockey*

"Ten more seconds and I can clobber somebody."

> *Snoopy, getting ready to play hockey, with 10 seconds left in the national anthem*

"I'm kind of like the chaperon at a Catholic school dance. I just stick my head in and say, 'Leave some room for the Holy Spirit, kids.'"

Paul Stewart, NHL referee, on fights

"It's a lot like watching a barnyard and seeing which of the roosters is puffing up the biggest."

Paul Stewart, on his instinct for detecting when a fight will start

"I, for one, really don't have any concerns about fights. Seldom do you see anybody get hurt, and the cheering indicates to me that nobody minds much."

Andy Van Hellemond, NHL referee

"Actually, I feel kind of cool, because I get to wear my sunglasses all the time."

Jay Wells, on having two black eyes after a fight

FINALS

"You know you've come a long way when you look at the out-of-town scoreboards and there are no scores."

Wayne Gretzky, on being in the finals

"Some of these kids are almost too young to spell Stanley."

Brad Park, after seeing some of the younger players in the '85 Stanley Cup finals

FINES

"In my office, where I work every day."

Lou Nanne, telling Tom McCarthy where to find him after suspending him for showing up late for a playoff-game practice

"Don't worry, Gerry. We could never stay out as late as you did."

> *Brad Park, after Gerry Cheevers took over as Bruins coach and announced that players would be fined for curfew violations*

"Mine is not to wonder why. Mine is to just pay or die."

> *Harry Sinden, on paying over $5,000 in fines for fights involving Terry O'Reilly*

FINLAND

"I guess you can say we added some Finns to the Sharks."

> *Kevin Constantine, Sharks coach, on drafting five Finnish players*

"There's a lot of competition between the newspapers there. They would like to report it every time I go to the toilet."

> *Teemu Selanne, on his celebrity status in Finland*

"Last night I went to bed feeling like an elephant on the edge of a cliff tied to a dandelion."

> *Bob Berry, on rumors of his being fired*

"I look at my record and, geez, I should have gotten a raise, I think."

> *Gerry Cheevers, fired by the Bruins after compiling a 204–126–46 coaching record*

"Not everything in life is fair. If it doesn't work out for me, it doesn't work out. I'm not going to jump off a bridge or something."

> *Rick Dudley, just before being fired as Sabres coach*

"As a coach, you must always remember that when you're on your way in, you're on your way out."

> *Punch Imlach*

"I've been fired more times than Custer's pistol."

> *Tom McVie*

"I've been fired more than Clint Eastwood's Magnum."

Tom McVie

"We just had a golf tournament for ex–Red Wings coaches and had to rent three courses."

Harry Neale

"I'm just like any other coach in the NHL. I sign a multiminute contract."

Harry Neale

"I may be impetuous, but I'm not stupid."

Peter Pocklington, Oilers owner, on rehiring coach Timo Lickowski ten days after firing him

FISHING

"They say that's business. If that's the case, I don't want to be a businessman. I'd rather be a professional fisherman."

Bobby Carpenter, on off-season contract negotiations

"It's like we baited the hook a little too weak. What we now have is a 600-pound marlin swinging away with our line."

> *Lee Fogolin, after the Oilers easily beat the Blackhawks in the first two games of a playoff series, then saw Chicago come back to tie the series*

"Ah, swimming pools. Think I can find any fishing out here?"

> *Kris King, Winnipeg Jets captain, on rumors that the team would be moved to Phoenix*

FLAMES

"Every time I get lonesome, I go to Calgary for a few days to see the guys."

> *Bob Plager, executive for St. Louis, on all the ex–Blues players on Calgary*

THE FLOWER

"Is he scary or what? He's 38 and he still shoots 600 mph."

Vincent Riendeau, on Guy Lafleur

FLY ME TO THE MOON

"I may be the only guy who wants to go back to the six-team NHL when they rode trains to games."

Wayne Gretzky, on his fear of flying

"As a general manager, I know this move will certainly improve the outlook of our budget. But as a coach, I also know we're losing a good friend."

Harry Neale, before the Canucks got rid of their team plane

FLYERS

"Whenever I walked through that big, black door leading into the visiting locker room at the Spectrum, I thought I was walking through the Gates of Hell."

> *Mike Robitaille, on the days of the Broad Street Bullies*

"If the fans want pretty skating, let 'em go see an old Sonja Henie movie."

> *Fred Shero, defending the physical style of the Flyers teams he coached*

THE FOG

"Sometimes I don't think he knows the difference between Tuesday and Wednesday. And sometimes I think he is a genius who has us all fooled."

> *Scotty Bowman, on Fred Shero*

"I don't live in the fast lane. I live on the off ramp."

> *Fred Shero*

"If you looked inside Freddie's brain, you would find a miniature hockey rink."

> *Mariette Shero, his wife of over 30 years*

FOOD FOR THOUGHT

"All I get now are free burgers."

> *John Anderson, Maple Leafs player, after selling his hamburger franchise*

"I'm looking for guys you toss meat to and they'll go wild."

> *Harold Ballard, on his player-recruitment strategy*

"I'd make the team meals if it meant staying here."

> *Rob Cowie, L.A. King, asked if he minded shifting from defense to forward*

"I ended up smelling like a giant hot dog."

> *Paul Holmgren, after ketchup thrown by a fan went down his pants*

"It'll be nice to get some home cooking for the guys with wives, and for me to go over to their homes [to eat]."

> *Paul Kariya, on a Mighty Ducks homestand*

"I was in the NHL one day, I was a chili salesman the next."

> *Gord Kluzak, on becoming an adman for P.J. Big Beef Chili*

"Starting August 1, I don't order french fries with my club sandwich."

> *Mario Lemieux, asked if he worked out during the off-season*

"I swear he's going to miss a flight one of these days chasing a hot dog in the terminal."

> *Bob McCammon, on Vladimir Krutov's love of junk food*

"I can shoot, follow through, do anything I want to do. I can even pick up dinner checks as long as they're not too heavy."

> *Rick Middleton, following surgery on his shoulder*

"Gives us the home-food advantage."

Keith Primeau, on fans throwing
octopuses at the Red Wings games

"Why don't we call the Colonel and order a bucket of chicken. Maybe hamburgers. If you have a water bottle out there, let's have lunch."

Glen Sather, on water bottles being
put on top of the nets at the
Spectrum as a courtesy to the goalies

"It's like ham and eggs. The chicken makes a contribution, but the pig, he makes a commitment."

Fred Shero, on the difference
between contribution and
commitment

"You wouldn't realize just how many commercials on TV have to do with food. You start to notice."

Mike Stapleton, on the difficulty of
eating with a broken jaw

"We were throwing interceptions, and they were running them for touchdowns."

> *Bob Johnson, Calgary coach, on*
> *losing a game 7–1*

"We'd be just two wins away from the Super Bowl if we were playing in the NFL."

> *Doug MacLean, Panthers coach, on*
> *starting the season with a 13–5*
> *record*

"I thought there was some good tackling out there. I figure if they can practice with the Lions, we should be able to practice with the Vikings."

> *Pierre Page, on a fight-filled game*
> *with the Red Wings*

"I've got Americans. I've got Canadians. I've got Finns and Swedes and Czechs. If I ever get fired, I can always get a job at the United Nations."

Herb Brooks, as the Rangers' coach

"Europeans won't stand up for themselves. They're not brought up the Canadian way."

Don Cherry

"They talk about all the things the foreign players have brought to the game. Well, let's see, what have they brought? The helmet, the visor, the dive."

Don Cherry

"I saw Winnipeg and New Jersey the other night, and they were just skating around. It was like a tea party, like watching Sweden and Finland play."

Don Cherry

"In Europe, we build plays. Here, they try to break them up."

Sergei Makarov, contrasting European and NHL styles of play

"He's stocky with black hair and he didn't bring along a girlfriend with him. He'll probably take one home, though."

Harry Neale, on how Patrik Sundstrom didn't remind him of the typical Swedish player

FORWARD CHARGE

"There are two types of forwards in the NHL. Scorers and bangers. Scorers score and bangers bang."

Ken Dryden

"Up front, you don't have to think as much. That should help Dave."

Don Maloney, after his brother Dave was switched from defense to forward

FRIENDS

"Are you enjoying the game? Are you happy in front of your friends?"

> *Don Cherry, during a Boston win over the Islanders, to Islander Eddie Westfall, who had said he got his biggest thrill out of beating his old team, the Bruins*

"The Dionnes like people. I serve the first beer. After that, I ain't moving."

> *Marcel Dionne, on being sociable to friends and teammates*

"I'd go over to his house and cook for him and his wife or shovel the walk if that meant he would stay with us."

> *Chico Resch, attempting to entice Rob Ramage, the star of the Rockies, to stay with the team*

FRONT OFFICE

"They kept me in the dark and every once in a while opened the door and threw manure on me."
> *Gordie Howe, after likening his treatment in the Red Wings' front office to that given a "cultivated mushroom"*

"I'm an insultant. And I'm insulting to the best of my ability."
> *Bill Torrey, after stepping down as Islanders GM to be a front-office consultant*

GRANT FUHR

"He was born to be a goaltender. I'm sure he feels more comfortable in his hockey equipment than he does in his pajamas."
> *Mark Messier*

GAME DAY

"Goalies never enjoy a game."
> *Gerry Desjardins, asked how he*
> *enjoyed a game*

"I like everything about hockey except the game."
> *Glenn Hall*

"Playing hockey is the only job I know of where you get paid to take a nap the day of the game."
> *Chico Resch*

GENERAL MANAGERS

"Please don't make this a battle of wits, me versus George. He's obviously unarmed."
> *Bob Berry, on being fired as coach by*
> *L.A. general manager George*
> *Maguire*

"One of the parents of every GM is a vulture. If you're in a little trouble, they come circling."
Brian Burke

"When I was in the hot seat, I could always get killed. Now, in the backseat, I can duck."
Emile Francis, on moving from
Whalers' GM to president

"I think I'll draft the Stastnys' old man and the father of the Sutters and start a breeding farm. These are pretty good bloodlines."
Harry Neale, asked what would be
his first move as Canucks GM

"When I was coaching I was fat and in shape. Now I'm just fat. I'm in the far end of my obesity scales."
Harry Neale, on becoming
Vancouver's GM

"As a coach I had a nagging headache. As a GM, I have a migraine."
Harry Neale

"As a GM, it's really important to have a comfortable phone—one that looks nice and doesn't have too loud a ring. You're on it all day."

> *Harry Neale, on a GM's most important tool*

"My wife asked me, 'How could you be a general manager, you don't even pay the bills at home?'"

> *Pierre Page*

"The coach makes mistakes and the general manager has to remind him of them."

> *Craig Patrick, on being both the Rangers' coach and GM*

"Some of the other GMs were like vultures trying to pick the meat off a carcass."

> *Bill Torrey, Islanders GM, on having a bad season at the same time the team was being sold*

"What pitching is in a short series in baseball, goaltending is in the Stanley Cup playoffs."
Jack Adams

"The man in the net makes the difference. Without the goaltender, you don't have diddly."
Art Berglund, Director of National Team for USA Hockey

"I just made up my mind I was going to lose teeth and have my face cut to pieces. It was easy."
Johnny Bower, on deciding to be a goalie

"He's got two legs, two arms, and a mask."
John Brophy, Maple Leafs coach, asked if he did any scouting of goalie Jeff Reese before calling him up from the minors

"It's like a tradesman. You don't see too many cabinetmakers anymore these days. It's an art. It's a unique trade."

> *Doug Carpenter, Maple Leafs coach, discussing the effect of NHL expansion on the overall quality of goaltending*

"We goaltenders tend to be very proud bastards."

> *Gerry Cheevers*

"Yeah, I figure if I read enough about myself, my head will get bigger and I'll be able to stop more shots with it."

> *Tim Cheveldae, Red Wings goalie, asked if he was reading about himself in the paper*

"All of us in Washington can appreciate what goalies do—we have so many shots taken at us. I wish that as well as a gift jersey, you'd lend me a face mask for the next year or so."

> *President Clinton, receiving a jersey from the Rangers after they won the Stanley Cup*

"Gamble has faced more shots than you see at last call."

> *John Davidson, after Canucks goalie*
> *Troy Gamble faced 42 shots in a*
> *game*

"He was younger, so he had to be the goalie."

> *Phil Esposito, on his brother Tony*

"The pressure is unreal. Most of the goalkeepers, they feel the pressure. The only ones that don't worry are the ones too dumb to understand what's happening to them."

> *Tony Esposito*

"Well, at least it's a good way to break in equipment."

> *Grant Fuhr, on giving up a lot of*
> *goals after joining the Maple Leafs*

"It was a good news–bad news type of situation. The good news is that we won; the bad news is that my average is 9.00."

> *John Garrett, Canucks goalie, after*
> *winning the first game of the season,*
> *10–9*

"Quit while there is still time—at about 12 or 13 years of age."

Gilles Gratton, advice to kids who want to be goalies

"Sixty minutes of hell."

Glenn Hall, on goaltending

"If you're not thinking three or four or five plays ahead, you're not finding goaltending interesting."

Glenn Hall

"Playing goal is a winter of torture for me. I often look at the guys who can whistle before a game and shake my head. You'd think they didn't have a care in the world. Me? I'm just plain miserable before every game."

Glenn Hall

"It's the only way I can support my family. If I could do it some other way, I wouldn't be playing goal."

Glenn Hall

"Only Dunlop has seen more rubber than I have."

Dominik Hasek

"It's like parting the Red Sea. He gives them an opening, but most of the scorers wind up drowning."

Paul Holmgren, on a hot streak of Sean Burke

"The quintessential bad-luck position. Pucks can go off bodies, skates, bounce into the net."
Mike Liut

"No, but I considered putting both in at once."
Barry Long, Jets coach, asked after a bad loss if he considered changing goalies

"Goaltenders not only have to stop the shots, but players flying at them as well."
Harry Neale, on the hazards of the job

"Trying to get him to make a first move is like pushing over the Washington Monument."
Lester Patrick, on Frank Brimsek

"In hockey, a goalie does nothing that other people do. Except for his sweater, he even dresses differently, right down to his skates."

Muzz Patrick

"If a goaltender makes a mistake, the red light goes on over him. And believe me, some nights you get sunburned out there with the lights, burning so much over you."

Pete Peeters

"Goaltending is a normal job. Sure! How would you like it in your job if every time you made a small mistake, a red light went on over your desk and 15,000 people stood up and yelled at you."

Jacques Plante

"I got one thing to say, gentlemen. I didn't have a good night."

Terry Sawchuck, after giving up six goals in first game of the 1967 Stanley Cup finals

"Goaltending is to hockey like putting is to golf. It really has no relationship to the rest of the game."

Harry Sinden

"There is no position in sports as noble as that of goaltending."

Vladimir Tretiak, legendary Russian goalie

"In hockey, goaltending is 75 percent of the game. Unless it's bad goaltending. Then it's 100 percent of the game, because you're going to lose."

Gene Ubriaco

"Yes, and I also like jumping out of tall buildings."

John Vanbiesbrouck, asked if he liked facing 51 shots in a game

"The only job worse is a javelin catcher at a track-and-field meet."

Gump Worsley, on goaltending

"Being a goaltender is not a job that would interest any normal, straight-thinking human."

Gump Worsley

GOALPOSTS

"I want to thank my friends the goalposts for getting me here tonight."

> *Glenn Resch, after nine shots hit the Islander goalposts during a playoff series against the Penguins*

GOD BLESS AMERICA

"Face it, people in the United States would rather watch *The Rifleman* than a hockey game."
> *Don Cherry*

"America is a wonderful place. You have 15 brands of mayonnaise."

> *Lada Fetisov, wife of Viacheslav Fetisov*

"I like fun. I like Rambo. I like music. I like cars. And I like pizza."

> *Petr Klima, asked if he was excited coming to the United States and playing for Red Wings owner and pizza baron Mike Illtick*

"I don't think she'll have a damn thing to do with it. Kate Smith doesn't shoot pucks."

> *Bobby Orr, asked to explain the Flyers' amazing record in games before which Kate Smith sang "God Bless America"*

"Every time Noel hears a certain song, he just knows he's gonna be in for a real bad game. That song is the national anthem."

> *Bob Plager, poking fun at Noel Picard*

"I felt like I was punching the American flag."

> *Al Smith, on getting into a fight with Olympic goalie Jim Craig soon after the U.S. hockey team had won the gold medal in the 1980 Olympics*

"When I was playing, it wasn't the Blackhawk crest that bothered me. It was Bobby Hull's slap shot."

> *George Armstrong, asked if he as a part Indian was offended by the Blackhawks' logo*

"I've never been afraid of what I do, but when Bobby blasts one, he puts the fear of God in you."

> *Hank Bassen, longtime goalie*

"It starts off looking like a small pea and then disappears altogether."

> *Les Binkley, on Bobby Hull's slap shot*

"There are days when you just step aside and leave the door wide open. It is a simple matter of self-preservation."

> *Glenn Hall, on being a teammate of Hull and being forced to practice with him*

"He's so strong, he doesn't call the cattle in, he carries them in."

Gordie Howe

"After all he's done for all of us, all we should do is bow whenever he walks into the room and kiss his feet."

Stan Mikita

GOLF

"I sliced it. Bad habit from my golf game."

Martin Brodeur, after nearly scoring a goal after clearing the puck

"What am I supposed to do? Trade him for Lee Trevino?"

Bobby Clarke, on Flyer Todd Bergen, who said he was going to pursue a career as a professional golfer

"One of the nice things about golf is that nobody slams into you when you're in the backswing."

Pierre Larouche

"Having been with Pittsburgh the last few years, he would have had more than a little time to refine his golf game, while the rest of us were out winning Stanley Cups."

> *Kevin Lowe, on Moe Mantha, who had a four handicap playing for the Penguins before being traded to the Oilers*

"In golf, they say you're only as good as your last four-putt. It's like that in every sport—you've got to keep producing."

> *Terry Murray, Capitals coach*

GRAPES

"If Cherry were to take over the Boston Pops, everyone would play the tuba."

> *Kevin Dupont, sportswriter, on Don Cherry's inability to use talented players in a positive way*

"He has a big pair of lungs to fill."

> *Armand Pohan, on Billy MacMillan replacing Don Cherry as the Colorado Rockies coach*

GREAT EXPECTORATIONS

"At first I thought there were seagulls in the building."

> *Dean Kennedy, after being spit on by*
> *Kjell Samuelsson*

THE GREAT ONE

"What he does best is make you look bad."
> *Richard Brodeur, on Wayne Gretzky*

"Once upon a time we had a rough-and-tumble game where everyone took care of themselves. Then along came Wayne Gretzky, who had a credit card to get all kinds of records because he had a guy like [Dave] Semenko looking out for him."
> *Don Cherry*

"He just seems to disappear out there. I can't believe a man can hide on a sheet of ice that's 80 feet wide and 200 long, but he can do it. And when he does appear again, it's nothing but trouble."

Jacques Demers

"There's a record book for Wayne and one for everybody else in the league."

Marcel Dionne

"I skate to where the puck is going to be, not where it has been."

Wayne Gretzky

"I didn't know whether to check him or ask for his autograph."

Bill Houlder, after playing against Gretzky in his first NHL shift

"I sometimes think that if you part Wayne's hair, you'll find another eye."

Gordie Howe

"There's only one way to stop Wayne Gretzky, and that's to lock him in the dressing room."
Gordie Howe

"Gretzky can put a pass through a thousand legs."
Willy Lindstrom

"There's no way he's going to be stopped unless he's injured or someone kidnaps him."
Al MacNeil, former Flames coach

"To get as many goals this year as Wayne Gretzky got last week."
Don Maloney, asked about his New Year's resolution

"I just think people will look back and realize that they had an opportunity to come and see maybe the greatest sports figure in history, and didn't do it."
Bruce McNall, former Kings owner, on not selling out the Great Western Forum every night after acquiring Gretzky

"What amazes me is he never stops amazing me."
Mark Messier

"You can wrap your suspenders around him and he'll still get away."
Gary Nylund

"Is that luck or skill when I beat him in the face-off and his stick plays the puck off my shins for the tying goal? I guess his skill brings luck."
Joel Otto, on a Gretzky goal in a playoff game

"I understand the Washington Capitals are going to trade for Wayne Gretzky. What do you think it would take to get him—two first-round draft picks and the state of Texas?"
President Ronald Reagan

"What I wanted to know is how did he always know what the toughest play would be for the goalie to make."
Chico Resch

"You could wear driving gloves and catch one of his shots and it wouldn't hurt."

Chico Resch, on the amazing ability of Gretzky to score without having a powerful shot

"Was Wayne Gretzky sick?"

Larry Robinson, after being named Player of the Week

"He doesn't wear that number 99 for nothing. That's about the percentage of plays that he is going to execute successfully."

Larry Robinson

"What he does on the ice isn't taught; it comes down straight from the Lord."

Glen Sather

"What Gretzky did is the most unheard-of thing I ever heard of."

Glen Sonmor, on another of Gretzky's many spectacular plays

"What do the Canadiens and a skunk have in common? They both get crushed on the road."
> *Anonymous, after the Canadiens*
> *posted an awful road record in 1995*

"We are always lucky in the playoffs."
> *Jean Beliveau*

"It's like going out with a girlfriend. You don't know when you are going to kiss her, but you know you will and when you do, it won't be the last."
> *Red Berenson, on the Blues beating*
> *the Canadiens for the first time in*
> *23 tries*

"We sometimes have to hold closed meetings before a game to get ourselves interested."
> *Scotty Bowman, on the great*
> *Montreal team of 1976–77*

"In Montreal, you can't even have a bad practice."
> *Pat Burns, on the pressure of*
> *coaching in Montreal*

"Playing for the Canadiens is like getting a Harvard law degree. Montreal players know what it's like to win."

Chris Chelios

"That's more unusual than the record."

Ken Dryden, on the Canadiens management giving out champagne after the team set an NHL record by going unbeaten in 24 straight games

"I even like the guys I don't like. They're a terrific buncha bums."

Punch Imlach, on his fondness for all his players

"The other players on the team make you so hungry to wear the Canadiens sweater that once you do, you remember what it was like, and you don't ever want to take it off again."

Pierre Larouche

"No matter what they would offer, my sanity, my health, and my life are worth more to me."

Jacques Lemaire, on considering coaching the Canadiens again after his Devils won the Stanley Cup

"With the Canadiens, pride is installed even in the rat holes of the Forum."

Frank Mahovlich

"When you are the Canadiens, you cannot make excuses."

Henri Richard

HAIR IT IS

"That's a pigment of your imagination."

Mike Bossy, on his hair turning gray

"My decision to make goaltending a career must have something to do with it."

Eddie Giacomin, on having gray hair at the age of 19

"There are streets in the city where our rookies wouldn't even draw a second glance."

Rick Green, on the Canadiens' tradition of shaving the heads of all rookies

"It makes me look younger. I wish it made me feel younger."

Doug Mohns, on his toupee

"If he had another hair on his back, he'd be up a tree."

Kenny Reardon, Canadiens VP, on the hairy back of Maurice Richard

"He really ought to dye his hair. It's embarrassing to find yourself tangling with a gray-haired man."

Jim Schoenfeld, on the 39-year-old Henri Richard

"No, why should they? No one tells the bald guys to get a transplant."

Chris Simon, asked if he was ever told by the Avalanche management to cut his long hair

"Goalies are a breed apart, and Hall is apart from the breed."

> *Scott Bowman, on Hall's unique character*

HAT TRICK

"The security guards tried to throw the guy out of the building."

> *Terry Crisp, after one fan threw a hat on the ice to celebrate the Tampa Bay Lightning's first hat trick by Chris Kontos*

"I kept this one to go fishing in."

> *Pierre Plante, who picked up a brown hat from several thrown after a hat trick*

"A rat trick."

> *John Vanbiesbrouck, after teammate*
> *Scott Mellanby killed a rat in the*
> *locker room, then went out and*
> *scored two goals*

"I thought I was going to faint after the third one. I was in shock."

> *Mick Vukota, on getting a hat trick,*
> *a rarity for him*

HEIGHT REPORT

"I'm supposed to stop the puck, not beat it up."

> *Don Beaupre, on being a 5'7" goalie*

"First time I saw him, I thought he was a bellhop."

> *John Ferguson, on the very small*
> *Danny Berthiaume*

"It's good to see those little guys do well."

> *Theo Fleury, 5'7", after watching the*
> *5'4" Ian Woosnam win the Masters*

"What about Corey Millen? I could eat an apple off his head."

Theo Fleury, on the 5'6" Millen

"You know, that's bigger than I am."

Arthur Griffiths, 5'1" owner of the
Canucks, on the size-21 sneaker of
Shaquille O'Neal

"We could lock arms and stretch from one end of the rink to the other."

Willie Huber, 6'3", on joining 6'4"
Barry Beck in the Rangers' defense

"It's like connecting the Atlantic with the Pacific."

Eric Lindros, on the Flyers' defensive
pair of 6'5" Kjell Samuelsson and
6'3" Chris Therien

"The thing is, when you get knocked down will you get back up? This is a game a small guy can play."

Bobby Orr, discussing how size is
overrated in hockey

"If I can't make it in this game, Denis Savard said he'll let me be a jockey for one of his horses."

> *Darren Pang, the 5'8" Blackhawks*
> *goalie*

"I sign autographs for 12- and 13-year-olds bigger than me. I was always the kid in the front row of school pictures."

> *Darren Pang*

"I think our goalie scout must be the guy from *Fantasy Island*."

> *Darren Pang, 5'8", who played on a*
> *team with Jacques Cloutier, 5'7", and*
> *Alain Chevrier, 5'8"*

"I guess the best line is, I'm bigger than the puck."

> *Darren Pang, allaying concerns*
> *about his height*

"Where's the rest of your goalkeeper?"

> *Larry Robinson, on Pang*

"He'd be great in a short series."

> *Gary Smith, on the 5'5" Bobby*
> *Lalonde*

"The guys tell me I have nothing to protect—no brain, no pain."

> *Randy Carlyle, on not wearing a helmet*

"Aw, don't worry about that, Doc. If it happens, I could always come back as a forward."

> *Harold Snepsts, defenseman, after being advised by his doctor to wear a helmet to avoid brain damage*

HOCKEY BASHERS

"Hockey would be a better game if it were played in the mud."

> *Jimmy Cannon*

"It's the same as what Rhett Butler said to Scarlett O'Hara."

> *Howard Cosell, asked his opinion of the Oilers beating the Islanders in the Stanley Cup final*

"A fast body-contact game played by men with clubs in their hands and knives laced to their feet."

> *Paul Gallico, on hockey*

"I like all sports and I like to play them all—except ice hockey."

> *Shaquille O'Neal*

HOCKEY STICKS

"I love your company and I like your style, but this gift is so cheap, I hope you don't come back for a while."

> *Muhammad Ali, after being presented with an autographed stick by the Edmonton Oilers*

"I'd like to see the guy who does it have to stay out as long as the guy he hurt."

> *Gordie Howe, on stick fights in the NHL*

"I only have one goal in each stick."

> *Petr Klima, on why he breaks his*
> *stick after each goal*

"I took the stick home and burned it in the fireplace."

> *Chris Kotsopoulos, after two*
> *opposition goals went off his stick in*
> *a losing effort*

"The hockey stick is the great equalizer."
> *Ted Lindsay*

"There have been times when I was squeezing the stick so hard, maple syrup has come out."
> *Larry Robinson*

HOCKEY WISDOM

"The game of hockey itself is very easy. It's the thinking about it that makes it hard."
> *Carl Brewer*

"It may sound strange, but the sign of a good hockey team is garbage goals."
Brian Burke

"The game is an entertaining form of chaos, encased in glass and barely controlled."
Gerry Callahan, sportswriter

"It's not like football or baseball: In hockey if you do something to another player, you have to stand up and be counted."
Don Cherry

"There has never been a successful team that did not take the body."
Don Cherry

"Hockey's a funny game. You have to prove yourself every shift, every game. It's not up to anybody else. You have to take pride in yourself."
Paul Coffey

"Your power play can win you games and your penalty killers can save you games."
Emile Francis

"You don't have to be angry to be a good hockey player."

Eric Heiden, on controlled rage

"As long as they play this game on skates, you have to be able to skate to win. Personally, I'll take a young pair of legs over an old head any time."

Dick Irvin, longtime hockey coach

"I try for good players and I try for character. If necessary, though, I settle for the player."

Phil Maloney, former Canucks GM

"Emotion carries you a long way. But it's a short-term friend. What you need is a long-term companion like talent."

Tom McVie

"Pro sports is only winning and losing."

Mark Messier

"In hockey, teams that are committed enough, intense enough, hungry enough, can make more of an impact than baseball or basketball players can make with the same intensity."

Mike Milbury

"Hockey is a game of intimidation. Always has been. Always will be."
Bob Murdoch

"It's very interesting. The same guys make the same mistakes and then you bring in new guys and they make new mistakes."
Pierre Page

"Being a hockey player meant that my boyhood lasted a long time and I often asked myself what I was going to do when I grew up."
Bob Plager

"They got 5'5" white guys making a lot of money."
John Salley, NBA player, asked his opinion of hockey

"The hockey player must have three things planted in his head—hate, greed, and jealousy. He must hate the other guy, he must be greedy for the puck, and he must be jealous when he loses. Hockey players without those traits don't survive too long."
Derek Sanderson

"To avoid criticism, say nothing, do nothing, be nothing."
Fred Shero

"Arrive at the net with the puck and in ill humor."
Fred Shero, offering his hockey philosophy

"We know that hockey is where we live, where we can best meet and overcome pain and wrong and death. Life is just a place where we spend time between games."
Fred Shero

"Success requires no explanation. Failure presents no alibis."
Fred Shero

"Two out of every three goals you score come from checking. One out of three comes from sheer finesse."
Harry Sinden

"It's the attitude of the players, not their skills, that is the biggest factor determining whether you win or lose."

Harry Sinden

"If you can't beat 'em in the alley, you can't beat 'em on the ice."

Conn Smythe

"Hockey must be a great game to survive the people who run it."

Conn Smythe

"The way I approach it is every game is a new season. There are 80 one-game seasons, and I'm looking forward to the next season."

Gene Ubriaco, on surviving as a coach

"Basketball is the one sport that can truly be influenced by one man. Baseball and football can't, and hockey no one understands anyway."

Pat Williams

HORROR FLICKS

"The way I look, I'd be perfect for *Friday the 13th, Part 17*. I could be Jason."

> *Craig Ludwig, on practicing with a mask over his face*

"They think they're hockey goalies."

> *Patrick Roy, on why his kids are not scared by bad guys in horror movies*

HORSE RACING

"There's only one other athlete I'd compare him to—Secretariat."

> *Gerry Cheevers, on Bobby Orr*

"You may have the most beautiful horse in the world, but if he doesn't win on the racetrack, why keep him? You might as well have a mule if he wins."

> *Larry Robinson, on player trades*

"They shoot horses who start good but can't finish the race."

> Brian Sutter, Blues coach, on not
> getting excited about a six-game
> winning streak early in the season

"When Bill Shoemaker wins the Kentucky Derby on a mule, then I'll concede that you can win without the horses."

> Lou Vairo, former Devils assistant
> coach

HOTEL VISIT

"It was so small that when I stuck the key in the lock I broke the window."

> Tom McVie, describing a small hotel
> room he stayed in during his AHL
> days

"I just ordered room service."

> Rick Wamsley, on why he didn't leave
> the 18th floor of his hotel during a
> fire alarm

"When Gordie came into the NHL, hockey was a Canadian game. He converted it into a North American game."

Clarence Campbell

"The only way to stop him is to crowd him, throw him off stride. But nobody wants to get near Gordie Howe."

Kent Douglas, Maple Leafs defenseman

"Gordie Howe was not only the greatest hockey player I've ever seen, but the greatest athlete."

Bill Gadsby

"Back then, if I could have gotten the crow's-feet and a couple of teeth smashed in, I would have been the happiest kid in the world."

Wayne Gretzky, explaining how he idolized Howe to the point of wanting to look like him

"All I know is that when I'm 51, I won't be in the All-Star Game. I'll be in the Bahamas watching Gordie play in it."

Wayne Gretzky

"There are two weak teams in the league and four strong ones. The weak ones are Boston and New York, and the strong ones are Toronto, Montreal, Chicago, and Gordie Howe."

Dave Keon

"A goal, an assist, and a fight."

Keith Tkachuk, defining a Gordie Howe hat trick

BRETT HULL

"We would be the Quebec Nordiques."

Paul Cavallini, asked what the Blues would be without Brett Hull. At the time, the Nordiques were the worst team in the NHL.

"It's kind of like we carry the instruments and he's the lead singer."

> *Glen Featherstone, on what it's like playing with Hull*

"I'm not a grinder. If we had 20 players like me, we wouldn't win five games all season."

> *Brett Hull*

"If you keep a Brett Hull off the board, or a Wayne Gretzky, or a Mario Lemieux, it's more a case of them having a bad night, not so much what you do against them."

> *Brad Marsh*

I H L

"This is a league for the masses and not the classes."

> *Richard Adler, president of the Atlanta Knights of the IHL*

"In Imlach's case, they probably removed the
bladder and left the gall."

> *Anonymous, after the legendary*
> *tough-guy coach and GM had a*
> *gallbladder operation*

INJURY

"Tell him he's Wayne Gretzky."

> *Ted Green, after Oilers player Shaun*
> *Van Allen had a concussion, and*
> *forgot who he was*

"No, but eleven other guys did."

> *Gordie Howe, asked if he ever broke*
> *his nose during a hockey game*

"I think my doctor has named his yacht after me."

> *Gord Kluzak, on his many knee*
> *operations*

"If he can't play, we'll transplant part of his body to other players."

> *Lou Nanne, on Dave Langevin, who was frequently injured but played with heart and determination*

"No, I never have. It's pretty good, too, because the NHL record is three."

> *Harry Neale, asked if he had ever seen anything like it when one of his players injured both of his knees on the same play*

"We raced the other day and it wasn't a photo finish. It was an oil painting."

> *Bob Plager, Blues executive, after scrimmaging with Doug Wickenheiser, who had injured his knee*

"The photographer doesn't say 'give us your best side.' He says 'give us your least damaged side.'"

> *Brendan Shanahan, on doing a fashion layout for a magazine*

"The doctor told me, if I see two pucks, to take the one on the left."

> *Charlie Simmer, after returning from his eye injury*

"He can also stand on top of his roof and bring in TSN [the Canadian Sports Network]."

> *Bernie Stafford, Oilers therapist, on Kevin Lowe having a magnetic current on his cast*

"I guess the toughest thing to do in hockey the last two years is play left wing for the Chicago Blackhawks."

> *Orval Tessier, Blackhawks coach, on having four left wings injured over a period of two years*

"It's difficult to play hurt—in fact, it's difficult to play when you're healthy."

> *Garry Unger*

INSURANCE

"I'm an insurance policy. When you buy insurance, you never know if you're going to use it. If you need it, you're glad you have it. If you don't need it, then you wish you would have saved the money you spent on it."

> *Chico Resch, on being acquired by the Colorado Rockies late in his career*

"I'm in the insurance capital of the world. I'm the biggest insurance anyone could get for the last 20 games of the season and the playoffs."

> *Tiger Williams, after being released by the Hartford Whalers near the end of the season*

IQ TEST

"The number on your back could be mistaken for your IQ sometimes."

> *Eddie Johnston, who wore number 1, on his stupidity in not wearing a mask*

"The worst thing that could happen to a hockey player is that he starts to think. A hockey player is not smart enough to think."

Dickie Moore

"He's like the planet Jupiter. We know he's out there, but we're not sure what he's doing."

Pierre Page, on Nordiques
defenseman Bryan Fogarty

"I listened to Kenny, but he uses incredible words, and whenever I'd ask him a question, he'd start explaining and ten minutes later I'd forgotten what I asked."

Rick Wamsley, on asking advice of
Ken Dryden

ISLANDERS

"It's like a car. You have to replace a few parts. We need some new spark plugs, that's all."

Al Arbour, after the Islanders went
two years in a row without winning
the Stanley Cup

"I'm still in awe of all those players. To stop them is just the most joy I can experience."

> *Michel Dion, Penguins goalie, on beating the Islanders during their Stanley Cup years*

"I don't know if they take survivors or just prisoners."

> *Chico Resch, then a member of the Colorado Rockies, who were the victims of the Islanders' 15th straight win*

JAROMIR JAGR

"I'd have to be up another solar system to be able to get on their wavelength."

> *Kevin Stevens, asked if he had some of the same moves as Jaromir Jagr and Mario Lemieux*

"Postmen don't go out for a walk on their day off."
Aaron Broten, on why he doesn't
watch hockey on TV

"I don't know if you could say I enjoy playing, but I like what goes with it. It's a good job . . . a good living. It keeps you in shape and it helps you stay young."
Tony Esposito, at age 39

"It's the difference between getting up at 8 A.M. and going to work when I'm 40 or getting up at noon and playing 18 holes of golf."
Theo Fleury, on trying to get in
shape so he can make the big bucks

"Temptation rarely comes in working hours. It's in the leisure time that men are made or marred."
Fred Shero

"You've got to understand one thing about Mike. He comes with an expiration date."

> *Anonymous, after Keenan left the Rangers*

"You have one up on everyone if you can figure out what's going on in that guy's head."

> *Brett Hull*

"We practice so much, I felt like we were getting ready for the Tour de France."

> *Jocelyn Lemieux, on Keenan's tough practices*

"Every player he has will be critical of him, but every player wants to play for him and win the Cup."

> *Gordie Robertson*

"At his current rate, he will eclipse all past records for coldness, anger, and public humiliation."

> *Steve Simmons, reporter, after Keenan openly criticized several players on the Blues*

"I can deal with the devil as long as he wins."

Neil Smith, on working with Keenan

"I guess it worked out for everybody except the Blues."

Neil Smith, on Keenan's defection from the Rangers to the Blues and the Blues then having a bad season

KINGS

"How can it work when the two most popular things in town are jogging and helping your divorced friends move?"

Don Cherry, on why hockey is not successful in Los Angeles

"There are 800,000 Canadians living in the L.A. area, and I've just learned why they left Canada. They hate hockey."

Jack Kent Cooke, former Kings owner

"Not enough people believe in us. A lot of people figured we were just beach bums, surfers, and Hollywood stars. I guess we proved them wrong."

Marcel Dionne, after the Kings upset the Oilers in the first round of the '82 playoffs

"They've got everything down there in L.A. except the West Edmonton Mall."

Ted Green, on all the ex-Oilers playing for the Kings

PAT LAFONTAINE

"When he's really skating, all you can see is the vapor trail. Once he gets by you, the only way to get him is with a whaling gun."

Al Arbour, on Pat LaFontaine

"Every time he touches the puck, we all sit up a little straighter and hold our breath."

Don Maloney, on LaFontaine

"Sometimes he looks like he is playing against 50 octopuses."

> *Gary Nylund, on how the opposition tries to contain LaFontaine*

LANGUAGE

"I tried to tell Luc how to box in Bossy, but Luc speaks French and he didn't understand me, which is probably why it worked out so well."

> *Gerry Cheevers, after Luc Dufour did a great job in stopping Mike Bossy in the playoffs*

"Before, I could order toast. Now I can order toast with jam."

> *Marc Crawford, Nordiques (now Avalanche) coach, on his progress in learning to speak French*

"It's a good language to have, because if I meet an ancient Roman, just think of the great conversation I can have with him."

> *John Garrett, eccentric goalie, on learning Latin*

"All pro athletes are bilingual. They speak English and profanity."

> *Gordie Howe*

"Do you want to fight?"

> *Pierre Pilote, tough defenseman, on the first English words he learned*

"The beep is the same in French or English."

> *Vincent Riendeau, explaining why his English-speaking friends should not be intimidated by his wife's French-language message on the couple's answering machine*

BRIAN LEETCH

"Brian Leetch is such a good hockey player, I am tempted to leave him in all the time."

> *Roger Neilson*

LIGHTNING

"My daughter tells me that some of her high-school friends have even asked for tickets on the 50-yard line."

> *Terry Crisp, Tampa Bay Lightning*
> *coach, on Floridians learning to*
> *understand hockey*

ERIC LINDROS

"There's no one else in the league who's capable of scoring 50 goals and using you as a speed bump."
> *Shawn Antoski*

"You can drive a truck on this kid's backbone."
> *Brian Burke, on Lindros's toughness*

"Philadelphia should make the Hall of Fame in the Builders Category—they built the Nordiques, didn't they?"

> *Joe Curnane, Bruins assistant coach,*
> *on all the players the Flyers traded*
> *to the Nordiques for Eric Lindros*

"It's getting to be like a 25-cent novel."

> *Pierre Page, on the many rumors*
> *about Lindros being traded from the*
> *Nordiques*

"Maybe Lindros can play one half of the season with one team and the other half with the other team."

> *Rogie Vachon, on the dispute between*
> *the Flyers and the Rangers as to who*
> *would get Lindros*

LOCKER ROOM

"That's so when I forget how to spell my name, I can still find my clothes."

Stu Grimson, on the Blackhawks'
decision to display color pictures of
players over the locker-room stalls

LOSING

"If the day ever comes when I swallow defeat, I'll quit."

Toe Blake

"I don't know whether to call [NHL] Central Scouting or the FBI and file missing-persons reports."

Herb Brooks, on the dismal play of
the North Stars

"I've had a bagful of letters. I've heard from agents, brother-in-laws, uncles, fans. Everyone has the answer."

> *Pat Burns, on a Canadiens losing streak*

"Hockey was my life. This could be my death after life."

> *Gerry Cheevers, on a 3–9–1 start as Bruins coach*

"What we have is a highlights slide."

> *David Courtney, Kings publicist, on the team's highlight film after a bad season*

"I feel like General Custer, but he didn't have to watch the video on Monday."

> *Terry Crisp, after the Lightning were blown out by the Blackhawks*

"I think things went well, other than we lost the game."

> *Todd Gill, Maple Leafs defenseman*

"We took a David Copperfield—our whole game was gone."

Ted Green, after the Oilers lost a game 5–2

"We're like a golfer on a par-3 hole. There's a pond between us and the green. And right now we're not even thinking of the green. We're thinking about what part of the pond we're going to lose the ball in."

Bob Johnson, on a Flames losing streak

"It's just like rheumatism. You keep looking for a way to relieve the pain, or better still, find a cure."

Marsh Johnstone, on a Colorado Rockies losing streak

"This season it's almost been like having to carry a stack of encyclopedias up six flights of stairs some nights."

Mike Liut, on a tough season

"It's our chemistry. We're going to have lab tests to see if we can find something."

Bob McCammon, on a lousy Canucks season

"It's like the old Western films where the Indians are circling the fort and the cavalry comes to the rescue. Well, the cavalry ain't coming here."

Tom McVie, on coaching the Winnipeg Jets, who had the worst record in the NHL

"I slept like a baby. Every two hours I woke up and started crying."

Tom McVie, asked how he slept after a loss

"Last season we couldn't win at home, and this season we can't win on the road. My failure as a coach is that I can't think of anyplace else to play."

Harry Neale, on the Canucks

"They better get jobs running a lighthouse where nothing upsets you."

Harry Neale, on the Red Wings players blaming a loss on a long plane ride

"It's the moonwalk I don't like—you know, when you take one step forward and then slide back."

Terry O'Reilly, on a Bruins losing streak

"Some guys looked like they went to Antarctica on a tour. They looked like they were frozen solid and couldn't move for two periods."

Pierre Page, after a bad game

"Ask the pool players—it's not what you make, it's what you leave."

Pat Quinn, after a loss as Kings coach

"It's just like the Masters in golf. Nobody remembers who finished second. They only remember who won the tournament."

Gordie Roberts, facetiously urging his team to break the North Stars' record losing streak of seven games

"It's like being dead without being buried."

Gene Ubriaco, on coaching the Baltimore team of the AHL, which lost 21 in a row

"When my ship comes in, there will be a dock strike."

> *Gene Ubriaco, on that same team*

LOVE AND ROMANCE

"My wife."

> *Reijo Ruotsalainen, Rangers*
> *defenseman and bachelor, asked*
> *whom he would most like to meet*

MAIL CALL

"Our goaltending has been okay, but not something to write home about. If you're going to write home, you write 'send money, cookies, and help.' That appeals to everyone."

> *Herb Brooks*

"Awaiting further orders on who you want us to beat next."

> *Harry Neale, after Jets coach Tom*
> *Watt sent him a thank-you note for*
> *the Canucks beating the Blackhawks*
> *and helping the Jets in the standings*

"The Czech is in the mail."

> *Harry Neale, asked when*
> *Czechoslovakian Petr Klima*
> *would be joining the Red Wings*
> *for training camp*

MALAPROPS AND FRACTURED SYNTAX

"We have only one person to blame, and that's each other."

> *Barry Beck, after a Rangers loss*

"That was complicated, folks, so let's have a replay for all you fans scoring in bed."

> *Bob Kelly, hockey announcer*

"No ****ing way. You've all gotta be there."
> *Moose Lallo, International League coach, asked by one of his players if practice was mandatory*

"It's not so much maturity as it is growing up."
> *Jay Miller, asked if his improved play was due to maturity*

"It's the most unheard-of thing I've ever heard of."
> *Harry Neale, after the Capitals lost two games in a row in the final three seconds*

"Fortunately, I've had good success against this team, because I've had poor success against others."
> *John Vanbiesbrouck, on being 14–1 against the Canucks*

MAPLE LEAFS

"If you've only got a day to live, come see the Leafs. It'll seem like forever."
> *Pat Foley, Blackhawks broadcaster*

"Benching a star in Toronto is almost like shooting the prime minister."

> *Dan Maloney, Maple Leafs coach, on benching Rick Vaive*

"It's tough. I could read all the stories in the Chicago paper with my orange juice. Now I have to get up an hour early."

> *Ed Olczyk, on playing hockey for the Maple Leafs*

"Coaching that team is like having a window seat on the *Hindenburg*."

> *Bob Plager*

"I don't have any fear of tackling anything anymore. If the prime minister called today and asked me to take charge, I'd say, 'I'll be right over.'"

> *Gord Stellick, on being the Maple Leafs' GM*

"Just think of this as a three-hour flight with the Maple Leafs."

> *Gord Stellick, after smoking was banned at Maple Leaf Garden*

"If there was any more heat on me, I'd be Ted Bundy."

Gord Stellick, Maple Leafs GM, after a tough season

"We don't need any more spare parts."

Tom Watt, Maple Leafs coach, on calls for acquiring a top center

MARIO THE GREAT

"You don't. You can ride on his back, but unless you tie up these long legs of his, he always seems to find a way to get his stick on the puck."

Bob Bassen, asked how you stop Mario Lemieux

"Stop Lemieux. Stop Lemieux. Stop Lemieux."

Rick Bowness, Bruins coach, asked to describe the strategy he was using in a playoff series against the Penguins

"If Mario's not getting his three or four points a night, you think he's got a broken leg or something."

Rob Brown

"He looks like he's playing in an industrial-league game at one in the morning."

Don Cherry, on Lemieux's propensity for floating during his rookie year

"I'd spend six months behind bars to have him on my team."

Terry Crisp

"Not only would I take jail, I'd take bread and water."

Terry Crisp, amending previous statement

"I told Tony if you're talking about Mario Lemieux, then you can have my whole team and I'll start over."

Phil Esposito, Rangers GM, discussing a phone call to his brother, who was director of operations for the Penguins

"Yeah, and Cinderella is only in fairy tales, too."

*Randy Exelby, in only his second
game in the NHL, on trying to stop
Lemieux's point streak*

"Throw a net over him. Better yet, maybe we should shoot him."

Mike Gartner, on stopping Lemieux

"His paycheck."

*Gordie Howe, on what he liked best
about Lemieux*

"I have no sympathy for goalies. No sympathy at all."

Mario Lemieux

"I feel like Spud Webb going against Abdul-Jabbar when I'm shadowing Mario."

*Rick Meagher, 5'8", on shadowing
Lemieux*

"What we have here is Michelangelo, but he can't get up the ladder."

*Tom Reich, Lemieux's agent, on his
many back injuries*

"A fire hydrant could score 40 goals with him."
Luc Robitaille

"I grew up watching Bobby Orr. And Wayne Gretzky was phenomenal. But Mario is on another level."
Kevin Stevens

"I have said it before and I'll say it again. You're looking at the next scoring leader in the league when Wayne Gretzky decides not to be."
Warren Young, during Lemieux's rookie year

"Most of the time when you see him coming, you might as well bend over and kiss your ass good-bye."
Wendell Young

MASK

"It must have been hard for the mothers to dress their kids for goal and say, 'Now, go have fun.'"
Glenn Hall, on playing goal before masks were in common use

"Our first priority was staying alive. Our second was stopping the puck."

> Glenn Hall, on playing without a mask

"The mask gives you protection, saves you a few hundred stitches. But the best thing it does is hide your face from the crowd."

> Bernie Parent

"I already had four broken noses, a broken jaw, two broken cheekbones, and almost 200 stitches in my head. I didn't care how the mask looked. I was afraid I would look just like the mask, the way things were going."

> Jacques Plante, on introducing masks to the NHL

"If you jumped out of a plane without a parachute, would that prove you're brave?"

> Jacques Plante, asked if wearing a mask proved that he was afraid

"You can't be a goaltender and be afraid to get hit in the face. But you can't be a human being and not think about it."

> Jacques Plante

"My face is my mask."

> *Gump Worsley, asked why he never*
> *wore a mask*

"Would it have been fair not to give the fans the chance to see my beautiful face?"

> *Gump Worsley*

MASS TRANSIT

"I got to know the meaning of the saying that when a Long Island commuter dies, whether he goes to heaven or hell, he must stop at Jamaica."

> *Bernie "Boom Boom" Geoffrion, on*
> *the Long Island Railroad, which*
> *invariably stops at Jamaica*

"You guys are boring. I guess you're not allowed to cheer or whatever, but that's no way to watch a hockey game."

> *Eric Lindros, to a group of reporters, after watching several games from the press box*

"I believe every person was put on Earth for a reason. Mine was to sell newspapers."
> *Eric Lindros*

"It's a good step—a good step backwards."
> *Jean Perron, former Nordiques and Canadiens coach, on his job as a radio commentator*

"I want to be a coach, because it's the quickest way to the broadcast booth."
> *Brent Peterson, Hartford Whaler*

"Messier has only three speeds—fast, faster, and fastest."

Emile Francis

"It's like some guys talk about a diet. If he stands up and he's overweight, you dismiss what he says. But if he stands up and looks like Arnold Schwarzenegger, you pay attention."

Mike Gartner, on the leadership qualities of Mark Messier

"The measure of Mark's game is not in goals and assists. The statistic he cares about is number of Stanley Cups won."

Wayne Gretzky

"When Wayne was here, you knew that if he was on that night, you'd win. That's how it is with Mess this year."

Craig MacTavish, on Messier leading Oilers to Stanley Cup in 1990

"I call him a 747. When he's flying on the ice, he moves the air. He makes the rink look too small."
>> *Jean Perron*

"You play your best because you are afraid of answering to Mark."
>> *Dave Poulin, who played alongside*
>> *Messier during an NHL–Soviet series*

MIGHTY DUCKS

"One time I was told to go down the hall, past the picture of Cinderella, and turn left. Another time I was told to go upstairs and turn right when I saw Peter Pan."
>> *Jack Ferreira, Mighty Ducks GM,*
>> *discussing his first few days on the*
>> *job at Disney headquarters*

"We're not employees. We're called cast members."
>> *Pierre Gauthier, assistant GM of the*
>> *Mighty Ducks*

"I'm not working on a cure for cancer here. Last time I saw, the puck was the same size in Prince Edward Island as it was here."

> *Dave Allison, Senators coach, on the difference between coaching in the minors and in the NHL*

"When I was a kid, I used to pray to the Lord to make me a hockey player. I forgot to mention the NHL, and so I spent 16 years in the minors."
> *Don Cherry*

"You should see me grocery shopping. I buy those little bottles of orange juice, those little boxes of cereal. If anyone broke into the house and looked in the refrigerator, they'd think some wee little people lived there."

> *Glen Hanlon, on being shuttled between the NHL and the minors*

"Shorter runways. Buses have a hard time taking off on short runways."

> *Pierre Larouche, on the best part of being back in the NHL after a stint in the minors*

"I think next year we'll get one in Iceland instead. That is no further away. And besides, I'm told people live longer there."

> *Harry Neale, on the farm team of the Canucks, based in New Brunswick*

"What's so bad about the minors? When most companies let you go, they don't find another job for you."

> *Pierre Page*

"It's good to go to Peoria. They haven't caught my act there."

> *Bob Plager, one of hockey's funnymen on taking his act to the minor leagues*

"You're probably only a piece of meat everywhere you play, but at least in the NHL, you're prime rib."

Steve Richmond, after the Rangers called him up from the minors

MIRACLE ON ICE

"My wife was hoping that Robert Redford or Paul Newman would get the role, so then she could play herself. Me, I just wish I had the money Malden made."

Herb Brooks, on Karl Malden playing him in the movie version of the "Miracle on Ice"

"My bartender in St. Paul said I could have one free beer every day for the rest of my life. I asked if I could bunch them up every so often. He said no."

Herb Brooks, after the 1980 Olympics

"I knew we were in trouble when our team started applauding the Russians as they took the ice."

Herb Brooks, on the United States playing the Russians in an exhibition game before the Olympics

"Heroes? Vietnam Vets are heroes. The guys who tried to rescue our hostages in Iran are heroes. I'm just a hockey player."

Mike Eruzione, on being hailed as a hero after the United States won the 1980 Olympic gold medal in hockey

"I'd love to hit a few golf balls on that."

Mike Eruzione, admiring the White House lawn after meeting President Carter

"I can paint houses. Even if I become a bum, I can still go into a bar with that gold medal and tell stories."

Mike Eruzione, on his future after the 1980 Olympics

"I didn't play in the NHL, because I wanted to walk away a winner."

> *Mike Eruzione, on deciding not to join many of his Olympic teammates in the NHL*

"Do you believe in miracles?"

> *Al Michaels's famed call after the United States beat the Russians in the 1980 Olympics*

MONEY TREE

"I'll propose anything where I can make a buck."

> *Harold Ballard, summarizing his business philosophy*

"The bonus money for winning wasn't much, but I always needed it, or maybe I was just too dumb to know the situation was serious."

> *Turk Broda, one of the NHL's all-time great pressure goalies*

"The biggest heist since the Brinks robbery."
Herb Brooks, on Peter Stastny's
$700,000 salary with the Devils at
the end of his career

"I've never reported it, because the guy is spending about $200 a month less than my wife did."
Herb Brooks, after his wife's
American Express card was stolen

"We'd all love to have a lot of money in the bank. But I'm so poor, I can't afford to pay attention."
Doug Carpenter, Maple Leafs coach

"Not unless a key is missing on the typewriter."
Dave Hannan, asked if he expected
to make a million dollars in salary
arbitration

"My wife made me a millionaire. I used to have three million."
Bobby Hull

"Now, instead of calling some guy a ****ing jerk,
we'll call him an overpaid ****ing jerk."

> *Brad Marsh, on the NHL disclosing
> players' salaries*

"Forecheck, backcheck, paycheck."

> *Gil Perreault, on the secret of success
> in the NHL*

HOWIE MORENZ

"He could start on a dime and leave just a nickel
change."

> *King Clancy*

"The athlete who thrilled me most was a hockey
player, Howie Morenz, who was head and shoulders
above any other man who ever played the game."

> *Jack Kent Cooke, in 1969*

"When Howie skated full speed, everyone else on
the ice seemed to be skating backwards."

> *Elmer Ferguson, sportswriter*

MOST IMPROVED PLAYER

"You know, I could win that trophy ten straight years and still be a candidate the next."
> *Bob Plager, on the Most Improved Player Award*

MOTHER KNOWS BEST

"My mom thinks it's enough."
> *Jeff O'Neill, Whalers player, on his three tattoos*

MOVING OUT

"I've always rented furniture. And the stuff I did buy, it's all different colors from all the different moves I've made."
> *Brent Ashton, on playing for several teams during his career*

"It was pretty easy. It was just me and my clothes and my golf clubs."

> *Mike Modano, on the difficulty in moving from Minnesota to Dallas*

"It's like Zsa Zsa Gabor said about all her marriages: There was so little difference with all her husbands, she should have kept the first one."

> *Pierre Page, on the North Stars' intention to move to Oakland*

MUSIC TO MY EARS

"I don't mind the kid at all, if you can keep him in tune. Like a violin, he needs tuning up every once in a while."

> *Harold Ballard, after a shouting match between Rick Vaive and coach Dan Maloney*

MUSTACHE

"A mustache never lost a hockey game. Besides, they might make our guys look a little tougher."

Lou Nanne, on letting his players grow mustaches

NAKED TRUTH

"I was happy to have an attraction in our building that we didn't have to pay for."

Harold Ballard, on a streaker in Maple Leaf Garden

NERVES

"I was so excited on my first start, I would have made coffee nervous."

Dan Bouchard, on being traded to the Nordiques

"What most people don't know is that my underwear is wet before the game even starts."

Gump Worsley, in response to Bill Gadsby, who said following a pressure game that Worsley wasn't tested and that his underwear couldn't even be wet

KENT NILSSON

"I told people that when Kent had that bounce in the first period, stay in your seat. If he doesn't, then go get popcorn or beer or something."

Bob Johnson, on the enigmatic Nilsson

NORDIQUES

"How many Nordiques does it take to change a tire? Only one, but they'll all be there if it's a blowout."

Anonymous, on a bad Nordiques team

"We've been making more mistakes than the referees this year."

> *Michel Bergeron, during a bad season in Quebec*

"The problem in Quebec is that we make people happier when we trade them."

> *Pierre Page*

NORTH STARS

"We appreciate all the fans that are here, but we really respect the five or six who stayed with us all year."

> *Jon Casey, North Stars goalie, after their miracle run to the finals in 1991*

"I was looking for elephants in the hallway."

> *Randy Cunneyworth, Whalers player, on a promotion at North Stars games that involved a masked man who ran around handing out money*

"We have no one who makes you stand up and say wow."

Pierre Page, on the North Stars' lack of a great player

"We're just like A. J. Foyt. He worries about every corner. This whole year is a series of corners."

Pierre Page, on the changing fortunes of the North Stars

"If you're not talking about football here, you're not talking."

Pierre Page, on the popularity of hockey in Minnesota

"The Twins' '87 march to the World Series was improbable. What is happening to the North Stars is approaching the mystical."

Patrick Reusse, sportswriter, on the North Stars' run to the NHL finals in 1991, despite a 27–39–14 regular season

"We lost and a Canadian official said, 'Don't worry, Jack, it wasn't your fault. The kids just couldn't put the puck in the net.'"

> *Jack Donahue, Canadian Olympic basketball coach, on his team losing a game*

"Six feet behind the Moose's behind."

> *Clark Gillies, asked the location of his hometown of Moose Jaw, Saskatchewan*

"Canada is a country whose main exports are hockey players and cold fronts. Our main imports are baseball players and acid rain."

> *Pierre Trudeau, former Canadian prime minister*

"It seemed like Glenn Anderson scored while they were playing the national anthem."

> *Murray Bannerman, Blackhawks*
> *goalie, after the high-scoring Oilers*
> *beat the Blackhawks 11–2*

"They think Edmonton is Paris. Their idea of fun is going to a bar and getting hammered all night."

> *Jimmy Carson, on his Oilers*
> *teammates of 1991*

"Muckler's hiding behind Sather and making all that playoff money for nothing."

> *Don Cherry, on John Muckler, who*
> *co-coached the Oilers with Glen*
> *Sather*

"When you've had success, you want more. It's like you're an alcoholic and you just can't get enough."

> *Randy Gregg, on the Oilers' desire to*
> *keep winning the Stanley Cup*

"If they do leave, I wonder if they'd let me buy one of those Stanley Cup banners for my restaurant in Toronto."

Wayne Gretzky, on rumors of the Oilers leaving Edmonton

"We're like Pavlov's dogs. Win and get a bone. Lose and we get the leash tightened real tight."

Dave Lumley, on the tight reins of coach Glen Sather

"You go to dinner with these guys. They grab their glasses and all you hear is *clink*. They have their championship rings on."

Moe Mantha, on the championship atmosphere he felt in Edmonton after coming over from the Penguins

"If we win, I would relish it more if we beat the Edmonton Oilers. If we lose to Edmonton, then I would prefer that we played the Poughkeepsie Huskies. I want to win the Cup from somebody."

Rick Middleton, before the 1988 finals between the Oilers and the Bruins

"My math isn't good, but I think we just lost 20 Stanley Cups."

> John Muckler, after the Oilers lost
> Grant Fuhr, Randy Gregg, and Jari
> Kurri

"The last great dynasty was the Ming dynasty. Not us."

> Glen Sather, on the Oilers' Stanley
> Cup years

OLD–TIMERS' GAMES

"It's still the same old story. My head says yes, yes, yes, but my knees say no, no, no."

> Bobby Orr, on playing in old-timers'
> games

"They told me if I scored a goal, I might be the most valuable player and win a car."

> Bob Plager, after scoring a goal on
> his own goaltender in an old-timers'
> game

"When he was on the ice, he had the puck 50 percent of the time, and he was almost always on the ice. He absolutely controlled games. He was amazing."

Don Awrey

"Bobby Orr's like O. J. Simpson on skates."

Gary Bergman

"They called him Bobby, B.O., The Kid, or No. 4. For what he meant to us, they should have called him God."

Dan Canney, Bruins trainer

"Hockey is a team game. One man is not supposed to beat a whole team."

Rod Gilbert, after Orr scored seven goals in a six-game playoff against the Rangers

"I'm glad I won the award now, because I expect it's going to belong to Bobby Orr from now on."
> *Harry Howell, after winning the Norris Trophy for best defenseman in Orr's rookie year*

"When he goes by my bench, I turn away so I won't have to watch."
> *Punch Imlach*

"He was two steps ahead of anyone, and then after his knee injury he was one step ahead."
> *Brad Park*

"Yes, I guess you could say it was one of his best games—he's had about 70 of them."
> *Harry Sinden, asked if a game in which Orr had two goals and two assists was one of his all-time best*

"Bobby was a star from the moment they played the national anthem in his first NHL game."
> *Harry Sinden*

"He looks like Bobby Orr out there. Some nights however, he looks like iron ore."

> *Tom Webster, on Kings defenseman*
> *Rob Blake*

OT

"The stupidest idea. Are we turning this into a circus? The National Hockey League circus."

> *Brett Hull, on the idea of shoot-outs*
> *instead of overtime*

"When your team gets the first goal, it's sudden, but when the opponent gets it, it's death."

> *Dick Irvin, asked for his definition of*
> *sudden death*

"We fought a long time to get overtime in. Now we're going to try and get rid of regulation time."

> *Harry Neale, on the Canucks playing*
> *16 overtime games in only half a*
> *season*

"To me it doesn't make sense. Five minutes of overtime is like 15 seconds of sex."
Bill Torrey

OWNERS

"No. The owners took it all."
> *Nick Kypreos, asked if he had anything to declare when leaving the United States during the 1994–95 strike*

"Try to surround yourself with the best people available, and when the time comes when an important decision has to be made, seek their advice. Then ignore them completely and do what you want to do."
Bruce McNall, former Kings owner

PAIN IN THE . . .

"The biggest favor I'll do for Petr is kick him in the rear and wake up his brain."

Ted Green, on trying to motivate the often difficult Petr Klima

PANTHERS

"The reason we play so well up here is we know we get to go home afterward."

Brian Skrudland, on why the Panthers play so well in Canada

BERNIE PARENT

"I've played two old-timers' games. That's more than I played as Bernie Parent's backup."

Bobby Taylor

"We won't have a problem because I don't believe in bed checks. In fact, every time I tried one in the past I never lost a bed."

>*Herb Brooks, on the idea of bed checks for playboy Pierre Larouche*

"I don't need more Stanley Cup rings. I just need money, beaches, and girls."

>*Jaromir Jagr, on wanting to be traded to a California team after winning two Stanley Cups in Pittsburgh*

"Not true. I've switched to Minneapolis."

>*Gump Worsley, responding to accusations that he did all his training in St. Paul bars*

PENALTY

"If that comes down, you've got a game misconduct."

King Clancy, legendary player and ref, to Babe Pratt after Pratt threw a glove in the air protesting a penalty call

PENGUINS

"To get everyone in, we need 90-minute games."

Bob Errey, on the offensive talent of the Penguins in the early '90s

GILBERT PERREAULT

"When he winds up and heads up ice towards you, beads of sweat build up on your forehead, because you know what he can do."

Barry Beck, on Perreault

"This is a hump you have to get over, and it usually comes in the first series. You get over the hump and you're on a roll."

Al Arbour, on playoffs

"What burned me was that we hadn't even played the fourth game yet."

Scotty Bowman, Blues coach, told by a Canadiens official that it was no disgrace to lose the '69 playoffs in four straight to Montreal

"The longer we go in the playoffs, the bigger the boat."

Pat Burns, on the size of boat he was looking for at a boat show just before the playoffs began

"Smaller pucks."

Tim Cheveldae, Red Wings goalie, on what changes during playoffs

"I think I have been able to maintain my scoring pace while guys like Guy Lafleur have tailed off. I always get an extra two months of rest because we never make the playoffs."

> *Marcel Dionne, on playing for the Kings*

"Two franchises that have generated more red ink than red lights in their 24-year histories."

> *Jay Greenberg, sportswriter, on the improbable 1991 finals between the Penguins and the North Stars*

"I wish there were back alleys on Long Island so I could drive on them and nobody would see me."

> *Kelly Hrudey, after the Islanders were eliminated by the Devils in the second round of the '88 playoffs*

"You put your hand on the stove once and know not to do it again."

> *Kevin Lowe, on the Oilers continuing to use their upset loss in 1982 to the Kings to motivate themselves*

"One of the problems with a short series is that it's like a trip to Atlantic City—you're either lucky or you're not."

> *Bob McCammon, Flyers coach, on five-game series*

"There was some thought that this game, which began on Mother's Day, wouldn't end until Father's Day."

> *Harry Neale, after a long delay in Game 4 of the 1988 Bruins–Devils series because of a shouting match between referee Don Koharski and Devils coach Jim Schoenfeld*

"The playoffs separate the men from the boys, and we found out we have a lot of boys in our dressing room."

> *Neil Smith, Rangers GM, after the Rangers lost in the playoffs to the Capitals*

PLUS/MINUS

"I check the plus/minus every week, hoping
somebody will take it away from me. I'll probably
go to the grave with this record."

> *Bill Mikkelson, on his record for the*
> *worst plus/minus, set (-82) during*
> *the 1974–75 season*

POLITICS

"A great guy socially—that is, for someone who
turned Canada into a socialist country."

> *Harold Ballard, on Pierre Trudeau*

"Mike Keenan never promised these guys a rose
garden, but there they were being introduced in
the Rose Garden."

> *Jay Greenberg, sportswriter, on the*
> *Rangers meeting President Clinton*
> *after winning the Stanley Cup*

"I want to find out who this FICA guy is and how come he's taking so much of my money."

> *Nick Kypreos, during the Rangers'*
> *visit to the White House after the*
> *team's Stanley Cup victory*

"Was that Dana Carvey?"

> *Brian Leetch, after President Clinton*
> *called to congratulate the Rangers for*
> *winning the Stanley Cup*

POWER PLAY

"It's like an actor. Either you remember your lines or you don't. Our guys didn't look like they could remember two words."

> *Pierre Page, on the North Stars going*
> *nine games without a power-play*
> *goal*

"I know it was early because Rocket Richard had his eyes closed in the picture on the dressing-room wall."

> *Vincent Damphousse, on a 7 A.M. practice called by Canadiens coach Jacques Demers*

"I know my players don't like my practices, but that's OK because I don't like their games."
> *Harry Neale*

"I wasn't disappointed by the turnout for the practice. I was disappointed with the turnout for the game."

> *Larry Robinson, Kings coach, on an optional practice—for which few players showed up—before the team lost their next game*

"I'm not going to second-guess him, although I draw the line at bungee jumping."
> *Neil Smith, on Roger Neilson's unorthodox preseason practices*

"What for? I get enough practice during the games."

> *Gump Worsley, asked why he does not put more effort into team practices*

PUCK

"A hard rubber disk that hockey players strike when they can't hit one another."
> *Jimmy Cannon*

"When we've got the puck, they can't score."
> *Paul Coffey*

RANGERS

"My doorman won't even talk to me."
> *Barry Beck, on losing in New York*

"I'm just glad it wasn't Machete Night."

Bob Froese, after Rangers fans threw
plastic mugs on the ice on Mug Night

"It's the last team I haven't beaten. Of course, I beat them a couple of times when I played for them, but that probably doesn't count."

Glen Hanlon, former Rangers goalie,
in 1988, before he had registered a
win against them

"Congratulations to the 1939 Stanley Cup Champions, the Boston Bruins. The New York Rangers look good for next year, but if they don't win it, they might not win it for the next 50 years."

Jim Rooker, current baseball
announcer, during a game in which
the Pirates and Giants played in
their 1939 uniforms

"It's supposed to be their year every year."

Serge Savard, asked if 1992 was the
Rangers' year

"I will match them insult for insult. I was just waving them on."

> *Billy Smith, on giving the finger to the Rangers' fans*

"Not only do you have to win the Cup, you have to make sure you don't screw up the parade."

> *Ron Smith, former Rangers coach, on how difficult it is to be the team's head coach*

"All of us love playing in the Garden. The fans there are so ugly."

> *Duane Sutter, Islander, on the Rangers' fans*

"The Rangers."

> *Gump Worsley, Rangers goalie, asked what team gave him the most trouble*

"I asked him for a pardon."

> *John Tonelli, on the Islanders*
> *meeting with President Reagan just*
> *after Tonelli was arrested for drunk*
> *driving*

"People have the wrong idea about traveling in the NHL. When we go on a road trip to Washington, people just assume we head straight for the White House for dinner with Uncle Ronnie and Nancy."

> *Mike Vernon*

RED WINGS

"It ain't exactly Chanel #5."

> *Peter Cusimano, who started the Red*
> *Wings tradition of throwing octopuses*
> *on the ice during playoff games,*
> *commenting on how it affects the refs*

"A home game is like buying a ticket in the Michigan lottery—you don't know what you're getting."

> *Harry Neale, on the Red Wings'*
> *unpredictability*

"I'm glad to get out of Detroit. There were too many cats there. Lions. Tigers. Now I'm here by myself, just one Tiger."

> *Tiger Williams, after being traded*
> *from Detroit to Los Angeles*

REFS

"If there weren't boos from the gallery, I'd have known that they didn't appreciate it."

> *Bill Chadwick, referee, after*
> *receiving boos on the night he was*
> *honored*

"What are the criteria? When the moons of Saturn are in line?"

> *Pat Flatley, after a referee refused to*
> *look at a videotape of a disallowed*
> *goal, claiming it did not meet the*
> *criteria*

"The old habit was too deep within me. I forgot where I was and what I was doing."

Ching Johnson, a great player who became a minor league referee, after bodychecking a player during his days as a ref

"The game moves so fast that a fellow can whack a guy and a second later be ten feet away."

Andy Van Hellemond

"Somebody has to explain to me how a guy is supposed to whistle down Wayne Gretzky when what he really would like is his autograph after the game."

Andy Van Hellemond

RELIGION

"Anyone who thinks that God wins or loses games has to have an awfully weak mind."

Harold Ballard

"Would you trust him with your collection plate?"
*Terry Crisp, on tough guy Theo
Fleury, who was once an altar boy*

"It's better to give than to receive."
*Gordie Howe, asked for his definition
of "religious hockey"*

"We get compensation from God. Two miracles."
*David Rubinstein, Penguins
marketing director, on Penguins
defenseman Tom Edur joining the
Jehovah's Witnesses*

RETIREMENT

"Don't retire until they tear the sweater off your
back."
Bobby Clarke

"I'm going to play it by ear. When my ear feels like
my legs, I'm gonna quit."
*Wayne Gretzky, asked how much
longer he will play*

"I'm going to go somewhere where the housing's cheap and the fishing's great."

> *Glen Hanlon, on his retirement plans*

"Nobody teaches an athlete how to retire."

> *Gordie Howe*

"When a rookie asked me if he could take my daughter out on a date."

> *Reggie Lemelin, on when he knew it was time to retire*

"When they hired conditioning coach Mike Boyle and he called a meeting in the weight room, and I asked, 'Do we have one?'"

> *Reggie Lemelin, on when he knew it was time to retire*

"When I started to receive, along with my paycheck, my pension check, and it still didn't change my tax bracket."

> *Reggie Lemelin, on when he knew it was retirement time*

ROCKET RICHARD

"Sure he can be stopped. With a gun."
> *Sid Abel, asked if Maurice Richard*
> *could be stopped*

"When he came flying towards you with the puck on his stick, his eyes were all lit up, flashing and gleaming like a pinball machine. It was terrifying."
> *Glenn Hall*

"He could find a loose puck in a pile of coal during a blackout."
> *William Leggett, sportswriter*

RIVALRIES

"It's *Dynasty* and *Dallas* rolled into one."
> *Michel Bergeron, on the*
> *Canadiens–Nordiques rivalry*

"Now we've got someone our fans can really hate."
> *Phil Esposito, Tampa Bay Lightning*
> *GM, on the Florida Panthers*
> *franchise*

"If you put us in a foursome, I'd hate to see what happened if one lost a ball in the woods. Something could happen in there; he'd never come out."
> *Pat Price, Nordiques defenseman, on*
> *the Nordiques–Canadiens rivalry*

LARRY ROBINSON

"Larry's the type of guy you want as your next-door neighbor. When your mower comes back, it's nicer than when you gave it to him."
> *Michael Forbes, reporter*

"That's like eating a can of beans and asking which one gives you gas. Honestly, I couldn't even pick."
> *Larry Robinson, asked to describe his*
> *greatest thrill in 17 years in hockey*

ROCKIES

"I'm an oilman and I don't drill dry holes twice."
Jack Vickers, former Colorado
Rockies owner, on selling the team

PATRICK ROY

"It looks like I found my first baseman."
Tom Runnels, former Expos manager,
on the brilliant glovework of Roy

RUNNER'S WORLD

"I'm sure the players think I'm crazy, but that's their problem."
George Kingston, Sharks coach, on
running ultramarathons

THE RUSSIANS ARE COMING

"I'm sick and tired of that Communist [expletive deleted]. He sneaked out of a hole in the fence somewhere and now he shoots his mouth off."

> *John Brophy, Maple Leafs coach, on Miroslav Frycer, with whom Brophy did not get along*

"We used to see the Russians every four years. Now we see them every four minutes."

> *Don Cherry, on the frequent recent play between the Russians and NHL players*

"The scary part is a guy who doesn't understand me is doing exactly what we want. And some other guys who clearly understand me haven't got it yet."

> *Terry Crisp, on Russian rookie German Titov quickly picking up the Flames' system*

"I'd welcome it. Besides, if we hold it over there, I wouldn't have to make cuts. If I'm lucky, the KGB will solve that for me."

> *Terry Crisp, on the idea of holding*
> *training camp in the Soviet Union*

"He called me a Commie. I didn't like that."

> *Darius Kasparaitis, on why he fought*
> *with Rick Tocchet*

"This wouldn't happen in Russia."

> *Sergei Nemchinov, on an NHL*
> *lockout*

"No more beer. Nine and a half months now, no bottle. I am good boy now."

> *Roman Oksiuta, Oilers winger from*
> *Russia, explaining his improved play*

"Their game is almost like soccer, really. Our game is a combination of basketball and rugby."

> *Pierre Page, contrasting the NHL*
> *and Soviet styles of play*

"They can both help the team as long as they don't kill each other."

> *Sylvain Turgeon, on Devils teammates*
> *Viacheslav Fetisov and Alexei*
> *Kasatonov, two former friends who*
> *no longer get along*

"My mom said they got the newspapers and nobody believed I am playing with Wayne Gretzky."

> *Vitali Yachmenev, Kings rookie, from*
> *Chelyabinsk, Russia*

SABRES

"Buffalo's got a lot of great people, but you have to trudge through the snow to meet them."

> *Dave Maloney, on being traded to*
> *the Sabres*

"They've got the same people as last year, but not the same players."

> *Tom McVie, on the Sabres, who did*
> *not change their personnel yet*
> *drastically improved*

"We're making a silent movie."

> *John Muckler, Sabres coach, whose*
> *team was on a great winning streak*
> *at the same time the Bills were in the*
> *playoffs, headed to the Super Bowl*

"Well, the Sabres are going to have to do something to take the crowd out of the game."

> *Harry Neale, on the numerous*
> *Canadiens fans in Buffalo during a*
> *Sabres–Canadiens playoff game*

SAFE SEX

"I told them, don't blow them up and put water in them. They aren't toys."

> *Pat Burns, on providing condoms in*
> *the Canadiens' dressing room*

SASKATOON

"Who the hell wants to go to Saskatoon, anyway? I don't want to be taking dogsleds around."

Harold Ballard, on the prospect of an NHL franchise in Saskatoon

"Why would anyone want to go to Saskatoon? That's where God left his snowshoes."

Harold Ballard, on rumors of NHL expansion to Saskatoon

"We'll fold the team and sell the players before we ever move there."

Harry Sinden, on rumors of the Bruins moving to Saskatoon

DENIS SAVARD

"The thing I live in fear of most in life is making a Denis Savard highlight film. I don't even want to be seen in the background of one of his goals."

Joel Quenneville

"Schmitty will never be anywhere as successful a coach as I was. He'll never be able to look down to the bench when he was in trouble and holler, as I could, 'Milt get out there.'"

> *Lynn Patrick, who used to coach*
> *Milt Schmidt*

SCORING

"I looked at the tapes and it was like reading a Sunday-morning comic strip."

> *Al Arbour, on the Islanders winning a*
> *game 8–7*

"Scoring is easy. You stand in the slot. Take your beating. Shoot the puck in the net."

> *Phil Esposito*

"Quick, draw me a finish line, before the other guys catch up."

> *Ron Francis, leading the NHL in scoring after the first week of the season*

"But Al had a better second half than I did."

> *Glenn Hall, on outscoring defenseman Al MacNeil during the season two points to one. Hall had his two points in the first half of the season.*

"Geez, I hate to waste my goal in a practice game."

> *Craig Ludwig, on scoring in an exhibition game after scoring six goals in five seasons*

"You've got to go to the net if you want to score."
> *Tom McVie*

"I didn't even know it went in. I didn't even know who passed it to me."

> *Larry Melnyk, on getting his first goal after five years in the NHL*

"I think it was before the invention of color TV."
> *Gord Murphy, Flyers defenseman*
> *who scored two goals in a game,*
> *asked when was the last time he had*
> *done that*

"I haven't had a period like that since pee wee hockey. I don't want to talk about it too much, but my book is coming out soon."
> *Colin Patterson, on tallying two goals*
> *and an assist in one period*

"I was scared. I had forgotten how to celebrate."
> *Yves Racine, who, after scoring two*
> *goals all season, had the game*
> *winner in a playoff game*

"That was not me. I must have entered someone else's body."
> *Harold Snepsts, low-scoring*
> *defenseman, after making two assists*
> *in a game*

"They'll ask me how many goals I have. I just tell them I have as many as they do."

> *Billy Carroll, Islander, on fans asking him how many goals he had during a season in which he did not score*

"I'd get a penalty every so often so my mother would know I was still playing."

> *Pat Hughes, Oilers winger, on going two months without scoring a goal*

"Not true. I scored the other night in a singles bar down the street."

> *Terry Ruskowski, on not scoring in 31 straight games*

SECOND PERIOD

"It's between the beginning of the game and the end, so maybe we look at it as a rest period."

Ed Olczyk, asked why the Blackhawks give up so many goals during the second period of games

SENATORS

"What would you rather have me do—get some Senators?"

Neil Smith, responding to criticism of all the ex-Oilers on the Rangers

SHACK ATTACK

"Shackie can play all three forward positions, but his trouble is that he tries to do it all at the same time."

Punch Imlach, on the frenetic play of Eddie Shack

SHARKS

"I can't say I grew up watching the San Jose Sharks."

> *Pat Falloon, after becoming the first-round draft choice of the San Jose Sharks*

SHORTHANDED GOALS

"We'd like to decline the penalty if we could against these guys, but there's no provision in the rules for that."

> *Dan Maloney, Maple Leafs coach, after the Oilers scored several shorthanded goals against the Maple Leafs*

SHUTOUTS

"I don't have a lot, so it's pretty easy to remember."

> *Glen Hanlon, asked, after his 13th career shutout, if he remembers them*

"At this pace, I'll have to play until I'm 114 to catch Terry Sawchuck."

> *Glen Hanlon, after his 13th shutout.*
> *Sawchuck had 102*

"The most I can ever remember is one in a row."

> *Greg Millen, after his third straight*
> *shutout*

SLAP SHOTS

"It felt like somebody had turned a blowtorch on me. I couldn't sit down for a week."

> *King Clancy, on Charlie Conacher's*
> *slap shot*

"It's almost an illegal weapon."

> *Chico Resch, on Al MacInnis's slap*
> *shot*

SLASHING

"When men played the game—Gordie Howe and those guys—you would get two minutes for slashing."

> *Bernie Nicholls, on being fined $10,000 for slashing*

SLUMPS

"I'd kill for a win. We must have one. If there was a doctor in the house, the prescription for what ails us is victory."

> *Craig Billington, during a Devils slump*

"We looked like 20 guys who just walked off the street and were thrown together for a game."

> *Russ Courtnall, Stars forward, during an 0–6–1 team slump*

"I told the guys on the bench that I've got a bonus for four."

> *Wayne Gretzky, on a 16-game slump, getting only his third goal in mid-February 1993*

"It's like when you open a new jar of pickles. It's hard to get the first one out."

> *Gilles Hamel, on scoring slumps*

"When I play I feel like I'm standing on a freeway, watching all the cars whiz by, and hoping like hell I don't get hit by one."

> *Morris Lukowich, on a slump*

"I am not letting anyone out of here. I want them to suffer with me and the rest of the fans in L.A."

> *Bruce McNall, asked, during a Kings slump, if there were any trades pending*

"I'd rather come home and find my wife cheating than to keep losing games like this. . . . At least I could tell her to stop."

> *Tom McVie*

"They should be shot at dawn. They could bring in God, but I don't think he could keep the players from making mistakes."

> *Harry Neale, on the Red Wings*
> *giving up a 4–0 lead after having*
> *lost nine straight games*

"The symptoms are much like a flu bug—you get sick and it takes time and a lot of patience to get healthy again."

> *Harry Neale, on slumps*

"I have three little kids who have no idea we were in a slump. So when I came home, it was a delight. They didn't know Daddy's team was in the tank."

> *Harry Neale, during a Red Wings*
> *slump*

"We've been in a slump."

> *Roger Neilson, asked the reason for a*
> *Rangers losing streak*

"We're like a bunch of artists, painters, who go out to paint, but if the sky's not blue enough, they don't want to work. We have to find people who will paint today."

> *Pierre Page, during a North Stars slump*

"We're like turkey leftovers from the holidays. Everybody wants to pick over the bones."

> *Brad Park, during a Red Wings losing streak*

"Stay away from your wives."

> *Eddie Shore, on the admonishment he gave to players when they were in a slump*

"Probably the biggest thing is that I haven't been able to score any goals."

> *Petri Skriko, Canucks player, asked why he was in a season-long slump*

"You just do three things—don't turn on the radio, TV, don't read the newspapers."

> *Peter Stastny, on coping with a Nordiques losing streak*

"If it were raining soup, we'd all have forks."

*Tom Watt, Maple Leafs coach, on a
losing streak*

"Daddy, you're the best hockey player in the world except that you can't score."

*Clancy Williams, six-year-old
daughter of Tiger Williams, during a
scoring slump*

"It's hard for me to believe that something which doesn't make me sweat or my lungs burn will do any good."

*Tiger Williams, after trying
psychological help to get him out of a
scoring slump*

"Before when I used to feel lower than a whale's belly, I would just pack some gun shells and blaze away."

*Tiger Williams, on learning new
relaxation methods of breaking out
of a scoring slump*

"They call Reggie Jackson Mr. October. Smitty is our Mr. April and Mr. May."

Al Arbour, on Islander "money" goalie Billy Smith

"Give him $10,000 if he beats them and nothing if he doesn't, and he'd beat them."

Bill Torrey, guaranteeing that the Canadian national team could beat the Russian team with Smith in the goal

"When I want to win a hockey game or walk down a dark alley, I know where Smitty will be. He'll be there."

Bill Torrey

SNEAKERS

"They said I could keep the sweatsuit, but I had to make a save to keep the running shoes they gave me."

> *John Garrett, Oilers announcer,*
> *called on as an emergency backup*
> *goalie after not playing for five years*

"Back home, the only thing we had with a pump was the well."

> *Dave Tippet, Capitals winger from*
> *Saskatchewan, on sneakers with*
> *pumps*

SPEED

"Three guys would have birthdays before we'd cross the red line."

> *Brian Burke, on slow defensemen in*
> *Vancouver in the late 1980s*

"No, Gerry, I have the tailwinds tonight."

Yvan Cournoyer, responding to Gerry
Cheevers's request that he slow down
on the ice

"When everybody skates, everything comes easier."
Henri Richard

STAGE FRIGHT

"It's a chance for a shy person to be onstage."
Chico Resch, on goaltending

"I was so nervous, I thought I was out there with
no pants and no shirt in the first period."

Anatoli Semenov, member of the
Lightning, on facing his old team the
Oilers for the first time

"It's only fitting that after all the places the Cup has been in the last nine months getting banged around, that it gets to spend the night here with you."

> *Gary Bettman, giving the Stanley Cup to President Clinton*

"The money's great, the accolades are great, but all they [players] want is their name on the Cup."
> *Ken Daneyko*

"Why not? He's a good dog."
> *Clark Gillies, on his dog drinking from the Stanley Cup*

"It was the first time I've seen our customers eager to touch something besides our dancers."
> *Lonnie Hanover, owner of Scores, a New York strip club, on Mark Messier bringing the Stanley Cup there after the Rangers won it in '94*

"Nothing is permanent in this business until you have the Stanley Cup perched on the trophy shelf."
Tommy Ivan

"I tell you, it has its own personality. Like it's talking to you."
Mike Keenan, on the Cup

"People in the streets don't come up and ask how much money you make in the playoffs. They want to see your Stanley Cup ring."
Kevin Lowe

"This is the most peaceful feeling in hockey. It's light as a feather. I think I could carry it forever."
Lanny McDonald, holding the Stanley Cup after winning it with the Flames in 1989

"You finish first in the regular season and they give you this big cheese plate. Thanks, but we'd rather win the Cup."
Barry Melrose, former Kings coach

"The New York Rangers are celebrating their victory by traveling around the city carrying the Stanley Cup. And out of habit, many New Yorkers are throwing change in it."

> *Conan O'Brien*

"It looks like someone sat on it."

> *Phil Pritchard, Hall of Fame spokesman, on dents in the Stanley Cup after the Rangers won it*

STRIKE—OUT

"I hope they strike. I can make more money on rock concerts than hockey anyway."

> *Harold Ballard, Maple Leafs owner, on proposed strike in 1982*

"Well, that should be easy. We already have the sticks."

> *Dave Brown, on hockey players carrying signs in the brief '92 strike*

"The players keep talking about all their concessions. What they put on the table, you have to pick up with a pair of tweezers."

Brian Burke, NHL VP, during the 1994–95 strike

"I wasn't much of a school person. I never paid much attention. But when you go to union meetings and it's about your life, you really pay attention."

Tie Domi, during an NHL strike

"I'm the only one the lockout didn't affect."

Glen Healy, who rarely played as a backup to Mike Richter

"It's over, thank the Lord. Technically, since they're not referees anymore, I can say how bad they are."

Brett Hull, at the end of the 1993 referees' strike, on the replacement refs

"I'd play 42 doubleheaders if I had to, to go back to work."

Dave King, former Flames coach, on ending the 1994–95 strike

"Now I can sit back and watch the baseball strike on the big screen and the hockey strike on the little screen."

> *Jay Leno, on a Christmas present of a TV with picture-in-picture capability*

"Give the next expansion team to the players. I'm sure their philosophy of what to pay players will change."

> *Pierre Page, on how to end a hockey strike*

"I'm a terrible sign maker."

> *Bill Ranford, on problems the 1992 strike would present him*

STRONGMAN

"All you see are those big kookaloos. That's why the game looks like it's played by robots. They're all like trees."

> *Bobby Hull, on the NHL's need for little guys*

"One of these days he might fight somebody, but right now he just squeezes guys, like they were an orange."

Babe Pratt, Canucks executive, on strongman Jiri Bubla

SUPERSTITIONS

"Very scientific. We get the number combinations from fortune cookies."

Wayne Cashman, Lightning assistant coach, on the strategies behind juggling lines

"I have these all over my locker area—four-leaf clover, Jewish star, Chinese good-luck charm. I can't afford to offend anybody."

Phil Esposito

SUSPENSIONS

"No way. I'd rather lose you for five games than Al."

> *Scotty Bowman, after being told by Bob Plager that it was really Al Arbour who deserved a five-game suspension for bumping an official*

"That's pretty expensive. I'd have been better off to beat the daylights out of the guy, get a lawyer, and settle out of court."

> *Steve Smith, on his four-game suspension for slashing Denis Savard, which cost him about $50,000 per game in salary*

SUTTER BROTHERS

"He would probably bite off your nose if he thought it would help him get close to the net."
> *Dave Babych, on Brian Sutter*

"You mean I've got to change my name to C. Sutter? No, thanks."

> *Clark Gillies, on having great success being on a line with Brent and Duane Sutter*

"Put all six Sutters together and they don't weigh 200 pounds. They just play like they think they do."

> *Bob McCammon*

"I don't know who they are or which is which, so how can I hit them? They're half my size and they're all over the place."

> *Willi Plett*

"I pray for a tie."

> *Louis Sutter, when sons Ron and Rick of the Flyers played against Brent and Duane of the Islanders*

"Ron is like all the Sutter brothers—small—until they start measuring heart."

> *Joe Watson, on Ron Sutter*

SWITZERLAND

"Some of my players have told me they're surprised they don't have to show their passes at the blue line when they backcheck."

> *Simon Schenk, coach of the Swiss Olympic hockey team, on the tight security in Calgary, site of the 1988 Winter Olympics*

"Well, he better learn how to yodel."

> *Harry Sinden, on Joe Juneau, who had said he might play in Switzerland instead of for the Bruins*

SYSTEMS DESIGN

"System is a $1.50 word for everybody knowing his position."

> *Bob Berry, asked what system the Penguins were employing in Lemieux's rookie year*

"Hell, I don't even know if he speaks French."
Toe Blake, asked if the very quiet
Henri Richard spoke English

"I've discovered that the less I say, the more rumors I start."
Bobby Clarke, Flyers GM

"If I wasn't talking, I wouldn't know what to say."
Chico Resch

"I've got nothing to say and I'll only say it once."
Floyd Smith, Maple Leafs coach,
after a loss

"We'll have to go to dental records to make a ruling."

> *Brian Burke, NHL VP, on trying to determine if Gary Roberts knocked out Trevor Linden's teeth with a high stick*

"I've got only one tooth in my head, and that's the one that hurts me."

> *King Clancy*

"You're not really a hockey player until you've lost a few teeth."

> *Bill Gadsby*

"I eat them all. Hey, the teeth are going to go one way or the other."

> *Jaromir Jagr, asked what becomes of the thousands of Kit Kat bars fans send him*

"Do you realize that's almost $7 million per tooth?"

Jay Leno, after Mario Lemieux
signed a seven-year contract worth
$42 million

"I didn't know they allowed cannibalism in this league."

Jim Peplinski, after his finger was
bitten by Claude Lemieux

TELEVISION

"I learned from watching *Happy Days* on TV."
Jari Kurri, on how he learned
English

"Me on television is like putting earrings on a pig."

Stan Mikita, on pursuing a career as
a television announcer

TENNIS, ANYONE?

"If guys can't take a hit, they should go play tennis."

> *Bryan Marchment, Edmonton defenseman, on low hits*

THEY SAY IT'S YOUR BIRTHDAY

"I woke up figuring I was one year older, but I'll bet I aged 10 years that night."

> *Gerry Cheevers, after celebrating his 42nd birthday on the same day the Bruins lost 10–5*

"I am a Cancer. I was born on July 16."

> *Claude Lemieux, after being told by Coach Herb Brooks that he was a cancer on the Devils*

TIES

"Nobody wants a tie. The only time you want a tie is when you come from behind with the Canadiens."

*Bobby Clarke, on the great
Canadiens teams*

"We're like a football team that can't run the ball. We can throw the ball, but we can't run it. We can't grind it out."

*Pierre Page, explaining the numerous
ties of the North Stars*

TIGER IN YOUR TANK

"You can't hurt the son of a bitch, and you never know what he's thinking."

Harold Ballard, on Tiger Williams

"I want to play 10 more years—by then everyone in the league will be wearing dresses."

*Tiger Williams, on the NHL's
attempts to outlaw fighting*

BILL TORREY

"Had he been General Custer at the Little Big Horn, not only would he have won the battle, but he would have traded for the best two Indians."
Denis Potvin

TOUGH GUYS

"I was trying to make friends, but he's a hard guy to talk to. I'm not fluent in cement."
Kelly Chase, on tough guy Wayne Van Dorp

"There are more no-hitters in the NHL now than if Nolan Ryan was here."
Don Cherry

"If you find you can push someone around, then you push him around."
Gordie Howe

"Carriers of water don't chop wood."

> *Red Kelly, Maple Leafs coach, on the*
> *distinction between enforcers (who*
> *chop wood) and skaters (the carriers*
> *of water)*

"In business, you get so you love everybody. But in this game you have to be mean or you're going to get pushed around. I keep telling myself to be mean. Be mean."

> *Ted Lindsay, on coming back to the*
> *NHL after a three-year layoff*

"I had a broken shoulder, a broken instep, a broken hand, and a couple of hundred stitches on my face. I just wanted to keep the ledger balanced."

> *Ted Lindsay, a little guy who had to*
> *be tough*

"You can have a great washing machine, but it doesn't do a lot without an agitator."

> *Bob McCammon, after signing tough*
> *guy Randy Holt*

"It was very simple. No autopsy. No off day."

> *Bob Plager, on his playing days*

"I'll take the guy who gave him the two black eyes."

> *Glen Sather, on tough guy Link Gaetz, who showed up for the NHL draft with two black eyes*

"I don't think toughness can be equated with a fossil imprint on the boards when you hit somebody. Toughness is taking and giving a hit to make a play."

> *Ted Sator*

"Hockey is a contact sport for me. It's not the ice follies."

> *Dave Schultz*

"Tough guys never have and never will get the credit they deserve. There should be a goon Hall of Fame, that is how tough it is."

> *Dave Schultz*

"If you keep the opposition on their asses, they don't score goals."

> *Fred Shero*

"They go from crushers, to rushers, to ushers."
Glen Sonmor, on tough guys who think they're scorers

"A lot of goal scorers can't count to five. Us tough guys, everybody knows we've all got 10 times more upstairs."
Tiger Williams

"When I go to the rink I want to be known as a jerk. I want to be the biggest jerk in the league again this year."
Tiger Williams

TRADE OF THE CENTURY

"He looks like Secretariat racing at the state fair."
Don Cherry, on Wayne Gretzky playing with the Kings

"Hell, Alaska went for less."
Ken Denlinger, sportswriter, on what the Kings gave up to get Gretzky

"Sort of like Baryshnikov spending the rest of his life dancing in Nicaragua."

> *Mike Downey, sportswriter, on*
> *Gretzky in Los Angeles*

"It's like putting Meryl Streep in a Jerry Lewis movie."

> *Mike Downey, on Gretzky in Los*
> *Angeles*

"He is going to add the winningness that he had to the other Kings players."

> *Magic Johnson, on Gretzky*

"If I bought a baseball team tomorrow, I'd say where's Babe Ruth? And the answer would be, he's not around. I was lucky enough with the Kings that his hockey equal was playing in our age."

> *Bruce McNall*

"Thank God, I believe in life after death."

> *John Muckler, Oiler co-coach,*
> *reacting to the Gretzky trade*

"He's already pulled the hat trick. He's put hockey on page one in Los Angeles in August."

> *Jim Murray, on the Kings getting Gretzky*

"If you know anything about show business, you know you've got to bring the act to Broadway. No matter how good you are in Bridgeport, it's still Bridgeport."

> *Jim Murray*

"The Edmonton Oilers without Wayne Gretzky is like *Wheel of Fortune* without Vanna White."

> *Nelson Riis, Member of Canadian Parliament*

"We've had 97 percent and 98 percent capacity. I'd have used 99, but we're not using that number anymore."

> *Glen Sather, on rumors the Oilers weren't selling out their arena after the Gretzky trade*

"I guess it was kind of like going from Alcatraz to Sing Sing."

> *Brian Beck, commentator, on Michel Petit being traded from the Nordiques to the Maple Leafs, the teams with the NHL's worst records*

"I'm not that popular in my own house. I have a 15-year-old daughter."

> *Bobby Clarke, on the Flyers trading the popular and handsome Peter Zezel*

"I've packed some extra undies."

> *Paul Coffey, on rumors that he would be traded during the All-Star break*

"I wasn't happy that I couldn't sell my house after I was traded. But now I can move right back in."

> *John Cullen, on being traded back to the Penguins soon after the Penguins traded him*

"He wants a ham sandwich for a cookie."

Jim Devellano, Red Wings GM, on
Dave Poile, Capitals GM

"I don't want to end up as the answer to a Trivial Pursuit question—'Who is the only guy to play for all 21 teams?'"

Ron Flockhart, on being traded for
the fourth time at age 24

"It's all dreamed up in somebody's outhouse. It's manufactured bull."

Emile Francis, on trade rumors

"I wish I had all the frequent-flyer miles for the teams I'm supposed to be traded to."

Grant Fuhr, on being the subject of
hundreds of trade rumors

"I'll be sad to go, and I wouldn't be sad to go. It wouldn't upset me to leave St. Louis, but it would upset me to leave St. Louis. It's hard to explain. You'll find out one of these days, but maybe you never will."

Brett Hull, on possibly being traded
by the Blues

"It's a big change from planning your golf trip April 3 to being with a serious contender for the Stanley Cup."

> *Brian Lawton, on being traded from the last-place Nordiques to the first-place Bruins*

"When you're 20th in the NHL out of 21, you don't have any untouchables. The only untouchable is the owner."

> *Bob McCammon, on a rumored shakeup of the Canucks*

"That's always the kiss of death. Just buy a house and you're gone. I've only slept in it two nights."

> *Greg Millen, who was traded two days after buying a new house*

"When you're upstairs as the general manager, you're on the phone working off all the vultures who want to trade you a ****ing nothing for all your good players."

> *Harry Neale*

"There's the one where you'll give up your headache and get one of theirs in return, only you just don't know how bad."

Harry Neale, on trades

"Everybody's out to trade a rowboat for a battleship."

Bob Plager

"The team that gets the best of a deal is the one that gets the best player."

Sammy Pollock

"That's why we all wear numbers, so that when we're gone, they put another player in the jersey."

Larry Robinson, on being traded to the Kings after 17 years with the Canadiens

"If I were traded to a contender, it would be like stealing from someone."

Borje Salming, on possibly being traded to a contender after a long career with the Maple Leafs

"Once you feel in your gut a deal will help your team and you don't act on it, it's time to look for a new job."

Harry Sinden

"Moving-van trades, I call them, because the moving-van companies are the only ones who make out well. Neither team benefits."

Harry Sinden, on late-season trades

"I guess you have to be part farmer and shut the barn door at night to make sure what you got doesn't get away."

Mike Smith, Jets rookie general manager, on other GMs wanting his good players

"That's not true. At the league meeting in Orlando, I offered my room maid two used towels for two clean ones."

Neil Smith, responding to criticism that he did not make trades at the 1990 league meetings

"Anytime you say hello to Phil, you could be in danger of making a trade."

> Gord Stellick, on trade-hungry Phil Esposito

"After the three-o'clock deadline went by, I picked up my phone to see if it was still working."

> Ken Wregget, on the many trade rumors involving him

BRYAN TROTTIER

"He brought fire to the franchise, even though the fire burned mostly inside."

> Bill Torrey, on the quiet leadership of Bryan Trottier

"They say it makes them stiff and sore. I've seen the same guys sit in a card game in a train for five solid hours without budging from their seats. They don't complain about being stiff and sore then."

> *Toe Blake, on a new rule in 1965*
> *that required substitute goalies to*
> *wear full uniform on the bench*

"I was going to ask for number 99, but they gave me number 4. Oh well, I guess they thought I played more like Bobby Orr than Wayne Gretzky, anyway."

> *Charles Bourgeois, Blues defenseman*

"There's certainly got to be a lot of goals left in that old jersey. I know I didn't use them all up when I played."

> *Lou Nanne, on giving his former*
> *uniform number 22 to first-round*
> *draft choice Brian Bellows*

"I would get my team into a football stadium as a marching band."

> *Harry Neale, on the ugly Canucks*
> *uniforms*

"The off-ice officials'."

> *Steve Tuttle, Blues player, asked*
> *whose uniforms he likes the best*

WAIVERS

"I'm sort of like a former stake horse that was claimed for the cheapest price there is."

> *Butch Goring, on being picked up on*
> *waivers by the Bruins*

WEATHER

"He could play in a tornado and never blink an eye."

> *Jack Adams, on Turk Broda, one of*
> *hockey's most unflappable goalies*

"I wouldn't say it's cold, but every year Winnipeg's athlete of the year is an ice fisherman."
Dale Tallon

WEDDING DAY

"She said, I hope your playoffs end soon so we can have a nice summer together."
Jacques Demers, on his new wife, who knew nothing about hockey

"I'd like to thank Wayne Gretzky for having me as his best man. I've had more press in the last 11 days than I did in the last 11 years."
Eddie Mio

WEIGH-IN

"He's always been scrawny-looking. He's never going to be a Greek god."
Doug McKenney, Whalers strength coach, on Rob Brown

"He tried to put on 25 pounds of muscle. It looks like 25 pounds of Molson."

> *Pat Quinn, on Kings rookie Dan Gratton coming in 25 pounds overweight*

"Have another doughnut, you fat pig."

> *Jim Schoenfeld, to referee Don Koharski during a controversial playoff game*

WHA

"You don't go into business with people who tried to torpedo you. And that's what the WHA did to us."

> *Harold Ballard, on the World Hockey Association*

"Well, it did seem a little strange to discover that number 4 carrying the puck was Ralph Hespivari, not Bobby Orr."

> *Gerry Cheevers, on defecting from the NHL to the Cleveland Crusaders of the WHA*

"In my scoring-title years and my Stanley Cup years, I had to take a summer job."

> *Gordie Howe, on jumping to the Houston Aeros of the WHA for big bucks*

WHERE'S THE BEEF?

"There's a lot of beef on the outside and a little fillet in the center."

> *Brian Sutter, on the Blues line of big wingers Todd Ewen and Craig Coxe centered by 5'8" Rick Meagher*

WIMPS

"I guess we'll have to outfit our team with ballet tights so they can tiptoe around out there."

> *Al Arbour, disgusted after an Islanders loss*

"You could send Inge Hammarstrom into the corner with six eggs in his pocket and he wouldn't break any of them."
Harold Ballard

"Tomas Sandstrom is a backstabbing, cheap-shot, mask-wearing Swede."
Don Cherry

"This should be a man's world—men dealing with men. The new world is a world of parking tickets and regulators and show business."
Don Cherry

"I think Phil Esposito is a man ahead of his time. If they keep these new rules, the NHL will have a lot of women playing."
Ted Green, on the Lightning having a minor league female goalie

"Why should a guy with a half-a-million-dollar contract want to have blood dripping down his face or sweater or play with bruises? Hell, they won't even play with bruised feelings now."
Bobby Hull

"No one is going to win the Stanley Cup wearing skirts."

> *Bob McCammon, on the importance*
> *of toughness in hockey*

WINNING

"Hockey is like a water tap. It takes a while to turn it back on once it's been off."

> *George Armstrong, Maple Leafs*
> *coach, after two straight wins*

"It's not boring to be scoring."

> *Scott Bjugstad, North Stars player,*
> *during a winning streak*

"All I know is I have a job here as long as I win."

> *Toe Blake*

"Winning is the name of the game. The more you win, the less you get fired."

> *Bep Guidolin*

"They say you can't be a winner until adversity is staring you in the face. Well, right now, it's touching my nose."

Kelly Hrudey

"It's not how many you win that's important, it's how many you show up for."

Barclay Plager

"We've just won 15 in a row and you ask me who's playing bad. No one's playing bad."

Bob Plager, Peoria [IHL] coach,
after Blues GM Ron Caron asked him
for a breakdown on who was playing
well and poorly

"Teams that win drive to the rink at 60 or 65 mph because they're excited to get there. Teams that lose take their time. There's no rush. They go about 30 mph."

Chico Resch

"Win together now and we walk together forever."

Fred Shero

"Put the kids in with a few old pappy guys who still like to win and the combination is unbeatable."

> *Conn Smythe, on the secret to winning*

"You get paid to win. Anyone can get paid to lose."
> *Gene Ubriaco, former Penguins coach*

"I consider myself a hockey entrepreneur. It's not the goals and assists I score that count, it's the bottom line—and the bottom line is winning."
> *Tiger Williams*

WORLD HOCKEY CHAMPIONSHIP

"You don't put financial conditions on an opportunity to play for your country, especially if you're a player who spent half the season in the minors."

> *Alan Eagelson, on Richard Brodeur refusing to play in the World Hockey Championship unless certain conditions were met*

YOU GOTTA HAVE HEART

"A player must be able to skate, have hockey sense, be able to shoot—not necessarily be able to score—and have drive. If he has the first three without the drive, he goes to the minors."

Pierre Page

"You can have all the talent in the world, but if the pumper's not there, it doesn't matter."

Glen Sather, on Jimmy Carson

"We'll probably call the Mayo Clinic for about 18 heart transplants."

Orval Tessier, after the Blackhawks
lost 8–2 to the Oilers in the playoffs

STEVE YZERMAN

"That's like asking me if I'd trade my son Jason for the kid next door."

Jacques Demers, asked if he would be
interested in trading Steve Yzerman

"If I wasn't coaching hockey, then I think I'd probably be driving the Zamboni."
Tom McVie

"I don't think the coach likes me. He told me to stand in front of the Zamboni."
Snoopy

INDEX

251

260